# JUNIOR BODY BUILDING

# JUNIOR BODY BUILDING

## GROWING STRONG

MUSCLE STRETCHING/LIMBERING UP
AEROBICS/BUILDING-UP EXERCISES/WARMING-UP EXERCISES
WEIGHTLIFTING/EATING RIGHT

### R.V. FODOR & G.J. TAYLOR

 Sterling Publishing Co., Inc.   New York

# Dedication

For Craig Gambrel, who's growing up strong

# About the Authors

R. V. Fodor has long been active in physical fitness training and has the know-how to guide any young person through growing up strong. An authority on strength building, Fodor is the author of several books and articles on nutrition and weightlifting, such as *Competitive Weightlifting*, published by Sterling. He lives in Raleigh, North Carolina, with his two young children (who are especially active in swimming) and his wife.

G. J. Taylor obtained his expert knowledge of using aerobics for physical fitness well before the nation's running craze took hold. An avid runner, Taylor lives in Albuquerque, New Mexico, in a household of young gymnasts.

*10·82 Pub. 8.29*

All photos by R. V. Fodor, unless otherwise specified.

Copyright © 1982 by Sterling Publishing Co., Inc.
Two Park Avenue, New York, N.Y. 10016
Originally published under the title "Growing Strong"
© 1979 by Sterling Publishing Co., Inc.
Distributed in Australia by Oak Tree Press Co., Ltd.
P.O. Box K514 Haymarket, Sydney 2000, N.S.W.
Distributed in the United Kingdom by Blandford Press
Link House, West Street, Poole, Dorset BH15 1LL, England
Distributed in Canada by Oak Tree Press Ltd.
% Canadian Manda Group, 215 Lakeshore Boulevard East
Toronto, Ontario M5A 3W9
*Manufactured in the United States of America*
*All rights reserved*
Library of Congress Catalog Card No.: 82-50552
Sterling ISBN 0-8069-4168-5 Trade
            4169-3 Library
            7676-4 Paper

# CONTENTS

INTRODUCTION . . . . . . . . . . . . . 7

1 YOUR BODY AND MIND—THE RAW
  MATERIALS FOR STRENGTH . . . . . . . 11
  Major Body Parts . . . Mind and Attitude . . . Questions
  and Answers

2 GETTING LIMBER BY STRETCHING . . . . 23
  Loosening Your Upper Body . . . Limbering Your Lower
  Body . . . Key Points for Successful Stretching . . . Your
  Stretching Regimen for Growing Strong . . . Questions
  and Answers

3 DEVELOPING ENDURANCE WITH AEROBICS    33
  What Are Aerobics? . . . Increasing Your Stamina by
  Running . . . Get into the Swim for Better Endurance . . .
  Wheeling Your Way into Condition . . . Jumping into
  Shape . . . Hints for Any Aerobic Exercise . . . Key Points
  for Successful Aerobics . . . Your Aerobics Program for
  Growing Strong . . . Questions and Answers

4 BUILDING MUSCLE THROUGH SIMPLE
  EXERCISE . . . . . . . . . . . . . 67
  Strengthening Your Chest, Arms, and Shoulders . . . The
  Way to Strong Abdominal Muscles . . . Developing
  Strong Back and Leg Muscles . . .Strength Builders That
  Need Special Equipment . . . Key Points for Successful
  Strength-Building . . . Your Exercise Regimen for Grow-
  ing Strong . . . Questions and Answers

5 WEIGHTLIFTING—THE MASTERLINK TO
 STRENGTH . . . . . . . . . . . . 84
 How to Get into Lifting . . . Lifting Weights the Right
 Way . . . Strengthening Your Legs . . . Building Up the
 Back . . . Developing the Chest . . . Shaping Up the
 Shoulders . . . Activating the Arms . . . Key Points for
 Successful Lifting . . . Your Weightlifting Regimen for
 Growing Strong . . . Questions and Answers

6 EATING RIGHT FOR A SOLID FOUNDATION . 122
 Get Your Energy from Carbohydrates and Fats . . . There's
 Power in Protein . . . Staying Healthy with Minerals and
 Vitamins . . . Avoid Those Junk Foods . . . Key Points for
 Good Nutrition . . . Your Diet for Growing Strong . . .
 Questions and Answers

7 TAKING CARE OF THOSE SORE SPOTS . . . 132
 Sore Muscles . . . Sprains . . . Strains . . . Cramps . . .
 Blisters . . . Illness . . . Questions and Answers

 GLOSSARY . . . . . . . . . . . . 139
 INDEX . . . . . . . . . . . . . 142

# INTRODUCTION

The final days of the 1976 Olympics marked the close of a four-year period of intensive athletic training for young Bruce Jenner. The soon-to-be world-famous decathlon gold medalist had devoted four solid years to building strength and endurance in order to achieve the athletic acclaim that he did. Clearly it paid off. As a result of his training, Jenner became the undisputed master of the strenuous ten-event contest.

Jenner's accomplishment is a model example of how developing your physical condition can lead to enormous rewards. But much of what you achieve depends on when in life you become aware of the importance of sound physical conditioning. As you may suspect, there's more to Bruce Jenner's claim to athletic fame than only four concentrated years of training—his bid for that spot in the limelight began years earlier. Like so many of today's outstanding athletes, Jenner grew up strong. His body was being prepared for that decathlon event while he was a youngster.

A background for success in athletics does not develop overnight. Better-than-average sports ability and all-around physical conditioning and strength begin during youth—often as far back as the pre-teen years. Growing up strong and good athletic performance go hand-in-hand.

But what about those who'll never make athletics a major part of their lives? In fact, that is the case for most adults. As it turns out, the benefits of growing up strong are not restricted to those who pursue careers in athletics. A little work at developing strength when you're young actually shows benefits long before you choose a career. It may help you make the mid-school basketball team, or enable you to run in a local distance race, or even smack a baseball out of the park.

Strength and good physical condition make a difference in non-competitive athletic activities, too. A camping trip with day-long hikes is a good example. Those walks are much more fun if your legs hold out and if you're not panting all the way. The same applies for something as simple as throwing a Frisbee in the park. Running after those mischievous saucers is more enjoyable when it doesn't wear you into the ground.

Perhaps the greatest reward of growing up strong is that it provides you with self-confidence. You feel strong and healthy and able to accomplish anything you want. Without question, growing up strong can have a tremendous impact on how well you enjoy the years ahead. Whether your ambitions are to become a business-man, a physician, a professor, a salesman, or even a writer, your career will be more rewarding with a childhood and adolescence that emphasizes growing up strong. President John F. Kennedy, who recognized this some time ago, once said, "Physical fitness is not only one of the most important keys to a healthy body, it is the basis of dynamic and creative intellectual activity."

There has never been a time when the need for growing up strong was more important. Medical professionals today are concerned with the increase of heart disease, obesity, alcoholism, drug addiction, and even tooth decay. Many of these problems will be avoided in later years by those who have achieved the proper early development. Also, the increased opportunity for the participation of women in sports has created a demand for developing physical fitness among girls at early ages. And the emphasis on overall sports competition at the high school, college, and professional levels commands attention for achieving physical fitness among the young. The need for strong youths is even greater now than when President Kennedy founded the President's Council for Physical Fitness in 1961.

But what is the best direction for a youth to take in order to develop physical excellence? Just as there are dozens of roads to take for various careers, there must be almost as many different ways to grow up strong. And what sort of discipline, equipment, and money does a person need to begin this path to physical fitness?

These are some of the questions that this book answers in detail. Our intentions are to point out the several ways that you—be you male or female—can develop a physically sound foundation, and to guide you to selecting the course of training best suited to your interests and needs. This information is arranged by progressive age groups in the form of training regimens that can be followed continually up to adulthood and maintained throughout those years.

That's what this book is all about: developing physical fitness and strength in young people. Running, swimming, rope jumping, calisthenics, bicycling, and weightlifting are some of the activities for you to partake in for strength development during the growing years. This book explains how you can grow up strong, healthy and fit by making the proper physical activities part of your youthful years.

**Extraordinary performances demonstrate the value of growing strong.**

# Chapter 1

# YOUR BODY AND MIND— THE RAW MATERIALS FOR STRENGTH

## Major Body Parts

To grow up strong, you not only need to develop your muscles, but you have to know them. Being familiar with your muscle groups is the first step in learning how to strengthen them. And all this takes is being able to identify the major groups of the back, legs, chest, stomach, arms, and shoulders.

Important, too, is understanding that growing up strong takes more than just muscles. Your lungs, heart, and entire circulatory system have their jobs to do, and developing strength is actually a combination of the actions of all these body parts. And then there's your mind. It is, after all, your mind that you use to control your muscles and to determine how strongly you want to·develop them. So, how you think and what your attitude is has much to do with how far you'll come in building up your strength and endurance.

Let's first get to the heart of it all—your muscles. Muscles are organs made up of bundles of fibres attached at their ends to the bones throughout your body. There are several hundred different skeletal muscles in your body. With their ability to tighten

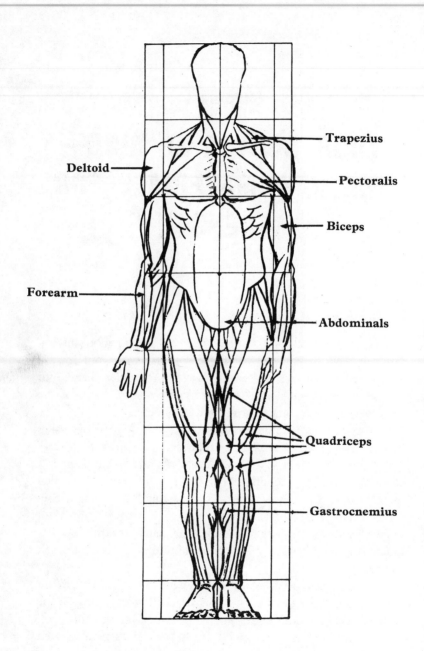

Trapezius

Deltoid

Pectoralis

Biceps

Forearm

Abdominals

Quadriceps

Gastrocnemius

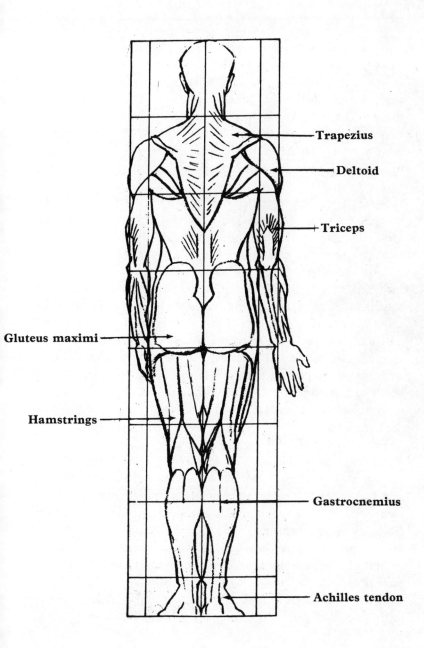

Trapezius

Deltoid

Triceps

Gluteus maximi

Hamstrings

Gastrocnemius

Achilles tendon

(contract) and to perform work, muscles offer you one of the most fascinating properties of life—freedom of movement.

In a very simple sense, muscles work because of certain chemical reactions in your body, largely involving oxygen, that permit them to contract. The greater the muscle movement, or contraction, the more oxygen is used. That's why a short run can easily leave you panting for more air. Your aim now is to make those muscle contractions become more powerful and more efficient as each year passes.

Some of the largest muscles are located in your back. There, the *trapezius* and the *latissimus dorsi* muscles are the most important members to develop. Luckily, most muscles have short nicknames and these two back muscles are better known as *traps* and *lats*.

It is the traps that form the upper section of your back, including the thick, padded muscles between your neck and shoulders. They control the raising and lowering of your shoulders and play a major role in your displaying good posture. The lats form two large triangular sections of muscle that cover most of your middle and lower back. If you raise an arm and then use your other hand to touch the muscle below your armpit, you will have located part of the lats. Your arm and shoulder rotations and your overall back strength depend greatly on the latissimus dorsi muscles.

Your legs also have huge muscle-groups. At the rear of your upper legs, or thighs, are the *hamstrings*. Below them are the *gastrocnemius* muscles, better known as the calf muscles (or just *calves* for short). The hamstrings enable you to curl your legs backwards, and the calves permit you to rise on the balls of your feet. Above the hamstrings are the muscles of the buttocks, known as the *gluteus maximi*. All these muscles are almost continually in action by the players of contact sports like football.

At the front of each thigh is a group of four muscles that are called the *quadriceps*. These muscles are important for bending at the knees. During running or when rising from a stooping position, you can feel the quadriceps come into play.

The large muscle-group located across your chest is known as *pectoralis major*. For short, these chest muscles are called *pecs*. Strength movements performed by the pecs include pulling your arms down towards your chest or pushing away from your body. This muscle group is especially important to swimmers.

Below your chest are the muscles covering your stomach, or abdomen. These are simply called the *abdominal* muscles, or *abs*. You test them out whenever you sit up from a prone position.

Perhaps the muscles most familiar to young men are the *biceps* of the upper arms. Flexing an arm to display the biceps has long been symbolic of one's strength. And there is actually some truth to that. The person with overall body strength commonly has well-developed biceps.

But when it comes to arm strength, the importance of the *triceps* is usually overlooked. These muscles, located behind the biceps, form over half of the upper arm and must be well developed for all-around arm power. And not to be forgotten are the muscles that encircle the forearms. In addition to contributing to arm strength, the forearm muscle group gives flexibility and strength to the wrists and hands. Making a fist will demonstrate the action of these muscles.

Finally, the *deltoids* are the muscles of the shoulders. Pushing, pulling and any rotation of the arms, such as throwing a football, brings the deltoids into play. They were also discovered long ago to make good cushions for hypodermic needles at doctors' offices.

Your respiratory and circulatory systems make themselves known any time you run hard or ride a bicycle uphill—you run out of breath and your heart beats faster. What happens is that your muscles are demanding more oxygen than your lungs are feeding them. But with enough hard breathing, your lungs begin to supply more oxygen to your blood, your heart pumps faster

A fast-paced game demands both strength and stamina from all your muscles.

to quickly carry the blood to your muscles and the muscles pull in the oxygen from the blood so that they can keep operating.

The respiratory and circulatory systems are not only closely linked together, but they share an equally strong bond with your muscle systems. Obviously, then, all-around strength includes strong lungs, a good heart, and solid muscles.

## Mind and Attitude

Strengthening your body parts takes determination—and that's where the mental aspect of growing up strong takes over. A person's mind has a tremendous influence on strength building and muscle performance. Sure, a track-and-field athlete may run with ankle weights to increase his leg strength and a baseball player will swing a weighted bat for developing added shoulder power. But neither of those special techniques will do them much good if they don't approach their game with the attitude that they *can* and *will* perform well, and that they'll continue to improve their athletic abilities.

In recent years, medical scientists and psychologists have come more and more to realize the importance of the mind in gaining and in improving athletic ability. As a result, many professional athletic teams in the United States, Canada and Europe now employ psychologists as sports behavioral scientists. These counselors are able to improve the mental attitudes of the team players so that they feel better about themselves, approach their games with healthy, winning attitudes, and apply their maximum physical skills throughout the competition. For example, baseball pitchers can be taught to maintain better control during high-pressure 3–2 pitch situations, quarterbacks can learn to compete better against the vanishing seconds on the clock near the end of the last quarter, and skiers can learn to help themselves to achieve faster downhill speeds while still demonstrating superb balance.

At this point in your strength career, however, our intentions are not to get you mentally prepared for outside competition. You may, after all, foresee no competitive activities during the coming years. In any case, it is still critical to realize the great effects mental attitude can have on your body. And this applies to your desire to grow up strong.

Perhaps most important for you is to display an eagerness to attempt new activities, yet understand that drastic physical changes will not happen overnight. The key attitude to acquire is one of perseverance—"sticking to it." You can't expect to run a mile non-stop, or even a half-mile, on the first day you jog. Nor can you expect to swim the width of the pool right at the start, or press a 55-lb. (25-kilogram) barbell over your head the first time you lift weights. Just as your growth takes place gradually over a period of many years, so does strength development. It is a slow process, but as long as you try it and stay with it, developing strength will become a steady process. *You* are your only competition for growing up strong! Much of the material that will lead to your success remains locked up in your head.

Remember, then, to always maintain that willingness to try. Never worry over your lack of ability in an activity that you have not performed before. You're sure to know other young people who can do more chin-ups, lift more weight than you, or are more flexible than you are. But never become intimidated or put off by the skills of others. With enough work at the same activities, you'll become equally good for your size, weight, and age. Here is where your determination to stay with your physical-fitness training comes in. Once on a particular strength-building regimen, stay with it because it will pay off in many surprising ways.

Besides self-encouragement to improve your body, avoid anything that harms it. And, as most people know, today's society provides plenty of opportunities to weaken the body you're trying to strengthen. Most notorious of these obstacles to strength are overeating, smoking, and drinking alcohol.

Overeating each day means you gain weight. But the weight you

**Growing strong means being able to perform your best in crucial competitive situations.**

put on is, unfortunately, useless fat. Scientifically, it is called *adipose tissue* and it collects beneath your skin. In addition to obesity taxing your body with extra weight to carry, more serious problems develop later—people who are fat when young tend to remain obese all their adult lives. Some of the consequences are heart disease, high blood pressure (*hypertension*), and kidney disease.

It is impossible to be in top physical condition if you smoke. The reason is simple—the smoke clogs your lungs and carbon monoxide prevents oxygen from entering your blood stream. When you exercise, then, your lungs can't supply all of the oxygen needed by your muscles. Worse than that, even if you work out regularly, smoking will prevent you from becoming as strong (especially in your heart-lung system) as you otherwise could.

Alcohol affects your physical performance in the same way that cigarettes do—it makes it difficult for hard-working muscles to receive oxygen. Advanced cases of alcohol consumption can lead to liver disease, and even to death.

It should be clear now that growing up strong is more than the development of muscles. Becoming strong requires participation from all your major body parts—including to a large extent, the material between your ears. Having an open mind and feeling good about yourself are as necessary for growing up strong as doing the strength-building activities themselves. Maintain a good attitude and you have won half the battle.

## Questions and Answers

*You only mentioned the importance of developing the major muscles of the body. What about all the dozens of smaller ones? Are they to be forgotten about?*

With this book's thorough presentation of body and muscle development, you needn't be concerned about missing any muscles. Usually, any attention you give to the major muscles will stimulate the lesser ones, also.

*I'm a 14-year-old girl and I plan to combine running 3 days a week with weightlifting. Will I develop bulging muscles in my arms and legs from these activities?*

Definitely not. In fact, your figure will improve because your muscles will be firmer and better-defined and you will probably lose any excess body-fat. Because of the female body chemistry, women generally do not develop large muscles.

*My gym class just took a physical fitness test. One of the events was a 600-yard (550-metre) run. I could barely run halfway and had to walk the rest. Does this mean I could never jog a mile?*

Certainly not. There are many people who jog a mile everyday, but can't run 4 miles (6.5 kilometres) at one time. You have to build up gradually, increasing the distance you run each week until you reach your goal.

*My interest is in competitive swimming, so I know I have to build up the pecs across my chest. Shouldn't this be enough for my purposes?*

By not exercising your whole body, especially your legs and shoulders in the case of swimming, you would only be cheating yourself of possible faster racing times in the near future. A strong swimmer is strong all over. Don't leave any weak links.

*My interests are just the opposite. I'm 15 and have no desire to compete, but I am concerned about growing up strong. My problem is that I have to work after school, which limits my time. Just how much time would I have to devote to physical fitness to increase my strength?*

Only a few hours a week; an hour a day 4 or 5 days a week is plenty for you.

*My best friend smokes cigarettes. He says I'm missing a lot and that it doesn't affect his health. Is he right?*

Pay attention when your friend climbs a couple of flights of stairs, or runs a short distance during any kind of field activity. He will surely be panting more than you are. And the more he smokes, the more he will pant and move farther from good health. You aren't missing a thing by not smoking.

Limber up! Keep your knees straight when touching the floor.

# Chapter 2

# GETTING LIMBER BY STRETCHING

If you've ever seen an alpine skier slalom downslope or a gymnast perform a floor routine, you know what it means to be limber, flexible and agile. A skier who is not loose would find himself down in the snow after the first slalom pole and a muscle-tight gymnast would be flat on the mat in no time at all. In sports, being limber makes the difference between winning and losing. But whether in competition or not, a person with tight muscles and stiff bone joints is just not in good shape. Because of that, he is far from reaching his maximum strength.

Stretching and loosening all of your muscle groups is the most fundamental part of any strength-building regimen. Just as a car's engine needs warming up before it can operate properly on cold winter mornings, your body requires exercises to gradually get it going at top speed. Without those warm-ups, you can damage a car's engine. Without loosening up through exercises, you're asking for the same sort of trouble—pains and strains. Injuries are not only painful and annoying, but they also prevent you from working out until the damaged muscles are healed.

Even though the main purpose of stretching exercises is to prepare an individual's muscular, respiratory and circulatory systems for more strenuous activities such as running or weight-lifting, they offer still more. By themselves, stretching exercises provide a special flexibility and agility that comes in handy whether you're dancing, cleaning the house or making a routine play at shortstop.

With less than a dozen basic movements, you can get every part of your body into a ready condition. To begin with, try each of the suggested movements. Later, when you decide to emphasize a particular strength-building regimen, work only on those most helpful or enjoyable. Near the end of this chapter, we suggest several groups for you to choose from.

If you're new at this, don't expect to be as flexible as the models in the photographs right from the start. Go slowly, both into the stretched position and out of it. Stretching is not a race. To receive the most benefit from each movement, use the best form you can, and where breathing is not restricted, hold yourself in the stretched position for several seconds.

You can do stretching exercises anytime and almost anywhere—perhaps the most convenient locale will be your living room. Remember, however, to wear loose-fitting clothing or material that stretches; go barefoot or wear sneakers.

## Loosening Your Upper Body

### Side Bends

One of the best ways to loosen your waist and stretch the muscles of your back and sides is to do side bends. Stand up straight and place your hands on your hips. For good balance, your feet should be about shoulder-width apart. Slowly bend to your right until you can't go any farther, being sure to keep your feet flat on the floor. Hold that bent position for about 5 seconds. Straighten and bend over fully to your left and remain there for several seconds. Do 10 to 20 side bends.

### Twisting

Like side bends, twisting stretches the muscles along the sides of your upper body and around your waist. In this exercise, however, these body parts are stretched in different directions than during side bends. Start your twisting by standing up straight with your feet about shoulder-width apart and your arms extended out from each side. Slowly rotate your upper body in one direction, keeping your feet fixed and legs straight. Move as far as possible and hold that position for about 5 seconds. Afterwards, rotate completely in the other direction. Repeat the entire twisting sequence 5 to 10 times.

A variation of this exercise is to do twists while holding a bar or pole (broomstick) across the back of your shoulders. The movement is done the same way as without the bar, but the extra weight and control in your outstretched arms enables you to stretch more fully.

## Kick-Over

You can stretch out and loosen your upper back and neck muscles with this kick-over exercise. Lie on your back with your arms extended along your sides, palms down. Slowly raise your legs up and over your head, trying to touch your toes to the floor behind you while keeping your legs as straight as possible. You may have to push with your arms to help boost your legs up and over. Don't be surprised if you're too tight at first to extend all the way back and over to make the touch. This exercise may take some working up to. In any case, extend as far as you can and hold there for several seconds. Do the kick-over 5 to 10 times.

## Bridge

Forming a bridge with your body is a great way to activate your stomach, chest, and back. Lie on your back with your hands above your head. Push with both your hands and feet to lift your stomach high off the floor. If you do it properly, only your feet and hands will be on the floor—and when you're especially limber, your legs will be straight. Hold the bridge for several seconds and do it up to 4 more times.

## Shoulder Rotations

Your shoulder muscles are usually fairly loose, but it's a good idea to be certain before you work at a more strenuous exercise, especially things like weightlifting, push-ups, etc. Stand with your feet shoulder-width apart and slowly move both arms (or one arm at a time) in circles, keeping them straight. You should feel a tugging on your chest, neck and back muscles, as well as loosening of the deltoids. Rotate each arm about 10 times. It's best to rotate them both frontwards and backwards.

One variation of this movement is to hold a bar with a wide grip and arms extended overhead. Gently push the bar behind your head to stretch your deltoids.

# Limbering Your Lower Body

## Toe Touches and Related Movements

It is important to loosen your hamstrings before playing almost any sport or, for that matter, before attempting any strenuous activity. These "leg biceps" are particularly sensitive to strains. The most direct way to stretch hamstrings is to do toe touches. Stand up straight with your feet 6 to 10 inches (15 to 25 cm) apart. While keeping your legs straight, bend down slowly and try to touch your toes. If you can't touch them, just reach down as far as possible without bending your knees and hold that stretched position for about 5 seconds. Stand up and repeat the toe touch about 10 times.

For added flexibility, combine back bends with toe touches. Lean over backwards as far as you can and remain there for a few seconds. Alternate toe touches are also useful for stretching your hamstrings and working them from a different angle. Stand with your feet fairly wide apart (wider than shoulder width) and with your legs straight. Reach down and over to touch your right hand to your left toes, without bending at the knees. Hold the position for about 5 seconds. Stand erect and repeat the toe touch to the opposite side. Do this movement 5 to 10 times in each direction.

Once you've mastered toe touches, you can increase your flexibility by touching your palms to the floor. This exercise is done the same way as the toe touch—reach down from the waist and remember to keep your legs straight. After placing your palms on the floor in front of your feet, hold them there for several seconds. Repeat the palm touch 10 times, with or without including a back bend in the movement.

An even more advanced exercise is to touch your head to your knees. If you can do this, you're practically guaranteed to have highly flexible hamstrings. As in the toe touch, reach down while keeping your legs straight, but this time grab your ankles with your hands. Then slowly bend farther, trying to touch your head to your knees, using your hands to help pull your head down. When you've gone as far as possible, hold for a few seconds and stand up again. Repeat 5 to 10 times. For variety, you can also do this exercise while sitting on the floor with your legs out straight in front of you. Simply lean over with your upper body.

Remember that you *must* work up to advanced positions slowly during a stretching session. Before putting your head to your knees, work into it gradually by first doing a few toe and palm touches.

## Leg Stretches

Many people prefer to stretch one leg at a time, rather than both together as in toe touches. To do this sit with your right leg bent to your side and behind you and your left leg straight out in front. Now grab your left ankle and slowly lower your head to your knee. Hold that lowered position for about 5 seconds. Repeat 5 times and then switch to stretch your right leg in the same manner. Like toe touches, this exercise also stretches the muscles in your upper back, but because of the way it thoroughly stretches the hamstrings, it is popular with track-and-field athletes.

A similar leg stretch can be done by sitting on the floor with legs outstretched in a "V" position. Bend over to touch one foot at a time.

## Lunge

This exercise will really give your quadriceps a good stretch. Place one foot well in front of the other and lower your body, bending at the front knee. Continue the movement until your rear knee touches the floor. At that point, your front knee should be well ahead of the foot. Hold for 5 seconds. Afterwards, recover to the starting position, place the opposite leg forward, and repeat the lunge. Stretch each leg about 5 times.

## Calf Stretch

Your calves must be kept limber if you're to maintain agility during any strengthening regimen. One of the best exercises for this is to stand facing a wall, bracing yourself against it with straight arms. Keep one foot about 2 to 3 feet (60 to 90 cm) from the wall and the other foot closer to it. Then, while keeping your back foot flat on the floor, slowly lean towards the wall. You'll feel a tugging in the calf farthest from the wall. Lean as far as you can, but if you go all the way to the wall too easily, start again with your back foot farther from the wall. Hold the stretched position for 5 to 10 seconds, then push yourself away from the wall to return to the starting position. Repeat 5 times with each leg. This exercise also stretches the Achilles tendon along the back of your ankle.

There are two popular variations of the calf stretch. For the first one, begin the same way, but have your back foot flexed so that the heel is off the ground. Slowly lower and raise your heel while keeping the rest of your body stationary. Repeat this 10 times with each leg.

The second variation is to do either of the two exercises just described, but keep your feet together so you work both calves at once.

# Key Points for Successful Stretching

- Wear comfortable clothes that are loose or that stretch as you stretch.

- Always move to the stretched position slowly. Jerky or rapid movements might result in pulled and strained muscles.

- Even when you're advanced at stretching, work into the difficult positions gradually.

- Hold the stretched position for at least 5 seconds. As you increase your flexibility, increase the time slightly. *Do not* hold the stretch for extended times if it interferes with your breathing.

- To achieve the most benefit, pay attention to your form. For example, you will not get much out of toe touches if you bend your knees while performing them.

- Be patient. Limbering up takes time. For instance, you cannot expect to touch your palms to the floor after doing only 1 or 2 sequences of toe touches.

## Your Stretching Regimen for Growing Strong

Stretching can be done every day, but it's not absolutely necessary in order to remain limber. Four good stretching workouts each week should be enough. It only takes about 10 to 15 minutes a day to go through a complete stretching routine—you could do it while watching television or listening to music.

Important to remember when doing your routine is to include some exercises that stretch your upper body and others that limber up your lower body. Keep in mind, too, the reason you're stretching your muscles on a particular day. Is it only to limber up, or is it to loosen up before doing a more strenuous activity? If you're warming up before running a mile, emphasize leg exercises. On the other hand, warming up for weightlifting requires stretching both your legs and upper body. Because the best warm-up exercises for specific strength-building activities are suggested in Chapters 3, 4 and 5, the routines below apply only to general limbering up. These may be on days when you're not going to exercise vigorously, but just want to achieve or maintain an overall agile condition. After a little experience with the movements, you may want to put together your own special routines.

Included below are the number of times, or *repetitions* (*reps*), you should do each movement. A group of reps is called a *set*. One set of each exercise is enough for a day's stretching.

Most of the regimens suggested elsewhere in this book are geared to fit your age. This is necessary because a 16-year-old, for example, should run farther or do more push-ups than a 10-year-old. But stretching exercises are different from strength exercises—people of any age can do them. In fact, some trainers believe that young people have an advantage. That is, the older the person, the harder he has to work to achieve fully stretched and agile muscles. But whatever your age, flexibility will surely come if you stay with a selected group of exercises.

## Routine 1

Side bends—5 to 10 reps on each side.

Toe touches, combined with back bends—10 reps.

Calf stretches—10 reps.

Leg stretches—5 reps each leg.

Kick-over—5 reps.

Shoulder rotations—10 reps each arm, each direction.

## Routine 2

Twists—5 reps in each direction.

Toe touches—10 reps.

Leg stretches—5 reps each leg.

Side bends—up to 10 reps on each side.

Bridge—3 to 5 reps.

Lunge—5 reps each leg.

### Routine 3

Leg stretches (straight-legged and V-style)—5 reps each leg.

Calf stretch—10 reps.

Kick-over—5 reps.

Side bends—5 to 10 reps each side.

Shoulder rotations—10 reps each arm, each direction.

## Questions and Answers

*I've never had any pulled muscles. Why should I do all the stretching exercises?*

You're lucky you haven't pulled any muscles—yet. As you get older and stronger, your muscles will become tighter and the possibility of injury becomes greater. Start stretching exercises now and avoid pain later.

*Why should the stretching exercises be done slowly? Won't you loosen up your muscles better by stretching them fast?*

If you do the exercises fast, your muscles will contract and not relax and become stretched. Doing stretching exercises fast means jerky or bouncy movements and that leads to straining your muscles—the very thing you're trying to avoid by doing the exercises in the first place.

*I've tried toe touches, but the backs of my legs hurt so much that I can't reach my toes without bending my knees. What can I do to improve?*

Be sure to keep your legs straight, even if it means not quite reaching your toes. Just stick with it. Get your hands down as far as you can and hold them there for 5 seconds. If you try every day, you'll eventually be able to put your palms on the floor.

*I can touch my toes, but don't come close to touching my palms to the floor, even though I work out every day. But I have a friend who can easily touch his head to his knees with his legs straight, and he rarely does any exercises at all. How can this be?*

Just as some people are naturally faster runners than others, some people are naturally more limber than the rest of us. You may just have to work a little harder. Again, stick with it and your legs will end up as loose as your friend's.

*Is any one time of the day better than another for limbering up?*

Not really. You'll probably find yourself tightest soon after you rise in the morning, but you can still loosen up as much then as you could later in the day. Also, wait about an hour after a meal before stretching.

*I've seen people do stretching exercises other than those you describe here. Is it okay to use such other movements in our routines?*

What we present are fundamental exercises—enough of the proper kind to provide you with a thorough loosening up. Feel free, however, to use as many other stretching movements as you like, as long as you go about them sensibly to avoid straining yourself.

## Chapter 3

# DEVELOPING ENDURANCE
# WITH AEROBICS

## What Are Aerobics?

When you watch the men playing in a professional football or
soccer game, you expect to see some of the strongest people
around. After all, these athletes make their livings using their
muscles. But there's more to their strength than muscle development—their strength includes endurance, or stamina, as well.
This is the ability to work your body hard for a long period of
time. Watch the players in a fast-moving basketball or hockey
game to see what endurance is all about. Or test your own
endurance by playing in a fast-moving game yourself.

People of all ages can develop better-than-normal endurance.
It may involve being able to run 2 miles (3 kilometres) nonstop, to
cross-country ski 5 miles (8 kilometres) straight, or to hike a 10-
mile (16-kilometre) trail up a mountain. In the water, good
stamina may show up as the ability to swim a mile ($1\frac{1}{2}$ kilometres),
and on a bicycle, stamina could be displayed by a 25-mile (40-
kilometre) ride.

Some athletes demonstrate superior endurance. Frank Shorter
and Bill Rodgers, for example, have run the 26-mile (42-kilo-
metre) marathon race many times. And Diana Nyad, the athlete
who tried to swim 100 miles (160 kilometres) from Cuba to

Florida, is another person with outstanding endurance. But most of us don't have the time to train several hours a day as these athletes do. Does this mean that we can't be as physically fit? Fortunately, that's not the case. Everyone can still develop good stamina without running or swimming such great distances.

What is the real purpose of having good endurance anyway, and how does it fit into a regimen of growing up strong? The answers to these questions lie in knowing the value of having a strong heart and efficient lungs. These two body parts form the cornerstone of good endurance and the foundation of great strength and health. By keeping your muscle cells well supplied with oxygen and free of waste products, your heart and lungs enable you to regularly increase the size and strength of your muscles. This may be through the aerobic exercises themselves, which are muscle-building, or through other activities such as weightlifting.

Like other muscles, the heart must be trained to become larger and stronger. The lungs must also be trained to provide all the oxygen your muscles need for long periods of time. Both heart and lungs must be able to work long and hard—to endure. A strong person not only has physically-fit muscles, he has stamina as well. This is where *aerobics* comes in.

Aerobics is the name for exercises that work the heart and lungs to increase their ability to perform. Running, swimming, bicycling and jumping rope are the best aerobics—but ice skating, roller skating, cross-country skiing, basketball, handball, and even disco dancing are good aerobic exercises, too. Without question, there are enough different activities to keep anyone active in any season, any weather, and any place.

The key to building up stamina is to regularly do an aerobic exercise long enough to get your heart beating faster than it normally does and your breathing heavier and deeper than normal. This heart-and-lung workout should last at least 15 minutes, nonstop. A few short aerobic sessions each week is all it takes to develop better-than-normal endurance and to establish the framework for muscular strength and good health.

The benefits of aerobics can be seen soon after beginning your regimen. One word tells it best: pep. But more than having energy, better endurance helps you to sleep better at night, lose body fat, and even perform better in the classroom or on a job. For example, a study has shown that when students who were not doing well in a Yonkers, New York, junior high school were started in physical-fitness training, their grades improved. And don't forget that most aerobic exercises also build muscular strength. Runners and bicyclists have powerful legs, and swimmers have chest and shoulder power.

Aerobic training brings these improvements to your body in several ways. Most importantly, it increases your lungs' capacity to gather oxygen, and your circulatory system's ability to transport the oxygen. The muscles used to fill your lungs with air become stronger, allowing more air to rush in with each breath. The number of red blood cells (which carry the oxygen from lungs to muscles) also increases. This greater number of red blood cells is carried by larger and stronger arteries and veins, and delivered to your muscles through a larger network of small blood vessels. And, of course, your heart becomes a stronger pump. The list of benefits from aerobics goes on and on. In short, aerobics help your body work better.

## Increasing Your Stamina by Running

Running is one of the most popular aerobic exercises. Millions of people make it the main part of their physical-fitness training. You can see them jogging through parks, on their local streets, on trails through the woods, along country roads, and around high-school tracks.

Although more popular today than ever before, running for stamina, strength, fitness and even survival goes far back in time. In the Stone Age, men ran after—and from—wild animals they needed for food. And during early historic times, running was an important part of life in ancient Greece, the site of the original Olympic games. In the first of these athletic events, held in the town of Elis, a foot race across the length of the stadium was won by a baker named Coeroebus.

Today, thousands of years later, the running tradition carries on. Not only is interest in competition still high, but more and more people run simply for the health, strength, and stamina gained from this kind of aerobic exercise.

Many magazines that specialize in running and related topics— such as the latest in running shoes and nutritious foods—are helping to increase the popularity of this aerobic. Among them are *Runner's World, The Runner,* and *Jogger's World,* and in England, *RACE, (Road and Country Enthusiast).*

We call this aerobic exercise running; others call it jogging. Still others argue that jogging is only slow running, but nobody agrees as to how slow. You can call it what you like. More important is that you take to the road as part of your physical conditioning.

### How to Get into Running

It would seem simple to begin an activity needing only an outdoor path. Just put on some running shoes, step outside, and you're on your way. To get the most out of running, however, it's not quite that easy. Even running requires some special attention.

Because your feet feel the weight of over 100,000 pounds (45,000 kilograms) with each mile you run, the most important piece of equipment you need is running shoes. A good pair of shoes is as important to the runner as the gloves are to hockey and baseball players. Buy a pair of good quality, one that is well-padded and has good arch supports. And be sure it fits well— not too snug, not too loose. You'll welcome the comfort that good shoes offer, especially as you increase the distance you run. Although running shoes may seem to be expensive, remember that a good quality pair will last for at least 1,000 miles (1,600 kilo-metres) of running. That's only pennies a week.

You should also take care of your feet by wearing thick wool or cotton socks. Besides providing extra warmth and soft padding, socks help prevent blisters and keep your feet dry. Be sure that you wear your running socks whenever you go to buy a new pair of running shoes.

Dress according to the weather when running, remembering to wear clothing that feels comfortable. Running clothes need not be expensive. You don't have to buy, for example, a special jogging outfit. Wear a T-shirt and shorts on warm days. On cool days, a sweat shirt, sweat pants, and perhaps a wind-breaker are fine. If it's cold, pack on more than one sweat shirt and add a pair of gloves and a hat to your clothing list. If you wear layers of clothing, such as two or three sweat shirts, you can remove some as you get warmer during your run.

Rain is a problem runners have to face. Some climates have at least a drizzle on half the days of the year. A warm, rainy day will not bother you much, and on hot days, you may even welcome a downpour. But for a rain shower on a cool day, wear a waterproof rain jacket.

One small item that you may find handy is an absorbent head-band to keep the perspiration off your face while running. And if you wear glasses, you may need an elastic strap to hold them snugly on your head.

When all set with the proper attire, you need only a place to run. Actually, this is one of the best points about running—you can do it almost anywhere. Some runners prefer a competition track so they can measure the distances they cover. Others enjoy a route with scenery, such as a country road. You can choose a path around a city park, a track on an athletic field, or the sidewalk around your block. Also, check your locale for any special trails or paths that some communities provide for runners.

No matter where you run, you may want to do it with a friend. A buddy system offers a companion to share experiences and helps maintain your enthusiasm. Also, doing any form of exercise with a friend is very helpful for making progress.

There are a few places to avoid during your workouts. One is busy streets and roads. Not only is the traffic dangerous, but you have to breathe exhaust fumes from all those cars and trucks. Smoggy air is both annoying and harmful. Others places to stay away from are rough trails through woods. As pretty as the scenery may be, the paths there can be filled with roots or fallen logs that are easy to trip over. So confine your running to smooth paths.

If you must run on or along streets and roads, be sure to protect yourself from cars and other vehicles—don't expect a driver to see you; get out of the way first. Run on a sidewalk or, if there is none, run on the side of the road facing the oncoming traffic.

The beach can be a great place to run—perhaps barefoot. The soft sand feels good underfoot and you might even splash through the shallow surf on hot days. Go easy at first, however. Your heels will sink into the sand, putting a strain on your Achilles tendon. This risks injury to a sensitive part of your ankle.

The weather presents some hazards, too. Extreme heat and humidity can lead to dizziness, nausea, headache, and possibly cramps. When it is unusually hot outside, run at a slower pace than you normally do. If you become tired quickly or extremely hot, or if you begin to perspire excessively, stop running. Cold weather offers its own set of problems, one of which is frostbite. This is a condition in which the cold causes crystals to form in the fluids and soft tissue of the skin. Toes, fingers, and ears are most susceptible, so take proper care to wear warm socks, gloves, and a hat. Fortunately, running makes your blood circulate efficiently to all parts of your body and prevents your skin from becoming too cold. Cold weather can also mean patches of ice on the ground and possibly a harmful slip. If there is too much ice, find another running route or wait until the weather warms up.

## How to Run Properly

How you run does make a difference. Whether you run for competition or for physical fitness and strength, doing it the right way is a must. Any other way can lead to injuries. You can strain your calves, Achilles tendons, knees, or lower back if you run incorrectly. Besides bringing discomfort, injuries can make it impossible for you to continue running regularly.

Although the differences in form among runners are not great, everyone does develop his or her own special style. To find your style, use comfort as a guide. This may mean taking shorter steps than a friend of the same height does, or perhaps placing your feet on the ground a little differently than others do.

Most runners follow a few general rules, however. The most important rule is that your feet should land about mid-heel and then roll forward to a flat-footed position. As your weight moves forward, you should move up onto your toes. It's a lot like walking,

*Photo by G. J. Taylor*

**Take steps in running that you find comfortable.**

except that you land more towards the middle of your foot when running. Some runners find the heel-first landing somewhat uncomfortable and prefer to land flat-footed instead. The flat-footed landing is also followed by the roll forward onto your toes.

Use the method that feels most comfortable to you. *Do not,* however, land on the balls of your feet or on your toes. This only puts unnecessary stresses on your heels, calves, and Achilles tendons. Also, your knees should be bent slightly with each stride to absorb the jolt of each landing.

Run with your back straight and with your body leaning forward slightly. Keep your head up and look ahead, not down at your feet. In short, run tall. Breathe naturally, gulping in all the air necessary to keep you going. You can keep your mouth open or closed, but you'll probably find that you can only get enough air by breathing through your mouth.

Arms have their proper place in running, too. Hold them loosely and relaxed at your sides. If you carry your arms too high, you'll only tire your shoulders and back. Don't clench your fists or swing your arms strongly as you might during a full-speed run. Both of these actions use up energy unnecessarily. Let your arms move with the natural rhythm of your body as set up by your steps, and keep your forearms about parallel to the ground.

## How Fast to Run?

To receive the most benefit from aerobic exercises, you must make your heart work harder than it normally does. You do not, however, have to work it to its limit. This means you shouldn't run as fast as you can, as you might when racing for a double during a baseball game or when competing in a 100-metre dash. Running at full speed does not really help your aerobic regimen because it prevents you from running long enough for your body to respond with increased stamina. Keep in mind that you need to run for at least 10 or 15 minutes without stopping. You cannot possibly run that long at top speed.

On the other hand, neither will you get much physical benefit from walking for 10 or 15 minutes. You must run a lot faster than you walk. A good running pace is one that allows you to cover a mile (1.6 kilometres) in about 8 minutes.

But each person really has to find the pace that's best for him or her. One guide is to note how you feel after your run. If you're not tired at all, you probably ran too slowly. Next time, increase your pace somewhat and see how you feel then. But if you're exhausted after running, especially if you remain tired for an hour or more, then you ran too fast. Slow down and enjoy a more healthful run your next time out. Another guide to use is that you should not run so fast that you couldn't carry on a conversation or sing a tune.

A scientific way to determine how fast you should run is to count heartbeats. First, determine how many times your heart beats in one minute while resting. Put the first two fingers of your left hand on the pulse in your right wrist to feel the beats. Second, count your maximum heartbeats in one minute, such as after a fast run. Then subtract the resting heart rate from the maximum number of beats. The best workout is the one that makes your heart beat at your resting heart rate plus 75 per cent of the difference between the high and low heartbeat numbers. Or, you could say that your workout heart rate should be equal to one quarter of your resting rate plus three quarters of your maximum rate.

For example, most young people have a maximum heart rate of slightly over 200 beats per minute, and a resting heart rate of about 75. (Both figures depend on age.) The difference between these figures (200 less 75) is 125. And 75 per cent of 125 is 95. When you add 95 to 75, you get 170. Or, one quarter of 75 is about 20 and three quarters of 200 is 150; 150 plus 20 is 170. A good pace, in this example, is one that makes your heart beat 170 times per minute.

Make your measurements using either a stopwatch or wristwatch that shows seconds. Many runners never leave home without one or the other. But if all this is too complicated, simply remember to run at a comfortable pace that leaves you tired, but not totally spent, for several minutes after the run.

For a check on the progress of your running speed, go to a measured track every once in a while and time yourself for a certain distance. Once a month is enough. All other times, just listen to your body to learn how you're coming along. With each week you should be feeling better, not only while running, but afterwards, too. When you feel good, you know you are running right.

### How Far to Run?

How far you run depends mainly on how much you've been running lately. It's unlikely that someone just beginning to run can run as far as someone who has been doing it for several months. As you build up your endurance through more and more running, you can run farther. The same applies to growing up. As you get older your endurance increases, reaching a peak somewhere around age thirty.

Whether a beginning or experienced runner, you should feel free to run as far as you want to. There's no limit, so long as you listen to your body. If you work too hard, it will be quick to let you know. When your body tells you that fatigue is setting in, slow down. Walk for a while if you need to, particularly during the early stages of your training.

There is, however, a minimum distance you should run. But rather than measuring it in distance, measure it in time. You should run for at least a certain amount of time—about 10 minutes to start with, and about 15 minutes after you run for a few weeks (slightly lower times for pre-teens). This will assure exercising your heart and lung systems and your leg muscles enough to strengthen them all. In terms of distance, this should be a little more than a mile (about 2 kilometres) to begin with, and about 2 miles (3.2 kilometres) later on.

# Get into the Swim for Better Endurance

Swimming is not only a good aerobic exercise, it's also one of the best all-around conditioners. Many activities call upon only one body part, but swimming uses and strengthens all major muscle groups. It gives your entire body a workout.

Originally needed by man for survival, swimming later became a sport and recreation in ancient civilizations. Both early history and mythology indicate the important role swimming had in Greece, Egypt, Rome, England, and Scandinavia. These early societies undoubtedly had contests to demonstrate athletic skills in the water, but the oldest written record of such an event dates back only as far as the 1600's in Japan.

Swimming remains a popular world-wide activity today. Although most of the millions of people who swim do so for recreation, many have discovered the value of using this exercise for physical fitness and for building strength. Olympic gold medal winners like Kornelia Ender of East Germany and Mark Spitz of the United States have helped increase the public's interest in the sport.

## How to Get into Swimming

It goes without saying that you must know how to swim before you can use the water for aerobic exercise. More than that, you should be skilled enough to swim steadily and safely for at least one-half minute. If you're a non-swimmer, take lessons. Even if you don't plan to use swimming as your aerobic exercise, learn to swim for safety's sake. If you do swim, but not well or properly, lessons will help you improve your technique and make swimming all the more enjoyable. You can call on the YMCA, a swim club, or your city's summer recreation agency to find out about lessons.

Where you swim depends mainly on what is available to you. Hopefully, you have access to an indoor pool because this is the best place for swimming as an aerobic exercise. The water is calm and

**Your swim suit should allow easy movement.**

warm, you can measure how far you swim, you can swim the year round and in any weather, lifeguards are on duty, and you're among other swimmers using the pool for aerobics. YMCA's and swim clubs are the likely places in your area that have indoor pools. You can also use the sea or a lake for aerobic swimming, but then you'll be limited by the weather.

Aside from water, you need little additional equipment. Your swim suit should fit well and permit easy movement through the water. Boys should wear snug-fitting trunks made of stretch material and girls a simple tank suit. For staying warm once you're out of the water, use a thick towel for drying and follow up by putting on a warm-up jacket or sweat shirt.

The chlorine in swimming pools and the salty sea water can irritate your eyes. If you find your eyes burning during and after swimming, wear a pair of swimmer's goggles. Young swimmers also sometimes develop "swimmer's ear," a bacterial infection in the outer ear canal. This isn't a serious problem and can be prevented by placing a few drops of isopropyl alcohol into each ear after swimming.

There's one safety rule for swimming that even the strongest and most skilled swimmers obey—*never swim alone*. Use the buddy system as a precaution against danger. Two or more experienced swimmers should always stay near one another and take responsibility for each other's safety. Trouble in the water usually happens unexpectedly, so having a friend nearby may save your life. Also be sure a lifeguard is on duty. If you're swimming in a new area, whether a pool, a lake, or the sea, become familiar with the surroundings. Learn how deep the water is, if there are any currents, and where the lifeguards are posted.

As with any exercise, *do not* precede swimming by eating a meal. Wait at least one hour after eating before taking a plunge. Working hard with a full stomach can lead to cramps, nausea, or just a plain bellyache.

If you develop or already have a special interest in swimming, you should know of several magazines: *Swimming World, Swimmers, Swimming Times* (England), and *International Swimmer* (Australia).

## Which Stroke to Use?

There are several styles of swimming, but competitors recognize only four. These are the *freestyle* (or *crawl*) stroke, the *backstroke*, the *breaststroke*, and the *butterfly*. All can be used for aerobic workouts. The most popular stroke, however, is also the fastest: the crawl, which is almost always used in freestyle events. This is the stroke where you lie face down in the water and pull yourself through it by extending your arms, one at a time, out in front of your head, as though you were reaching over barrels.

Knowing how to do more than one stroke, however, will add variety to your workouts and will exercise your muscles from different angles. The breaststroke is a second style that will make a good addition to your aerobic training. This stroke is one of the

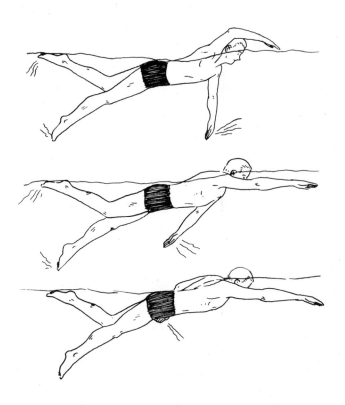

Here and on page 46 are the stages of the crawl.

Stages in the breaststroke.

easiest. It requires lying face down, using a frog kick, and keeping your arms underwater to push away from your chest.

Our intention here is not to equip you with outstanding swimming techniques, but to help you with an aerobics regimen once you know how to swim. On the other hand, if you are only a beginning swimmer, you'll find the following pointers helpful.

*Freestyle swimming*: Lie in the water face down with both feet extended straight back, and with one arm extended in the water above your head. Place your other arm along your side with hand at hip. The water level should be up to your forehead.

To begin, turn your face to the side opposite the extended arm to inhale, and start bringing the other arm along your side up and out of the water. Turn your face back into the water and begin to exhale through your nose. Extend the out-of-the-water arm, slightly bent, over your head as though reaching over a large barrel. Your arm should enter the water fingers first, followed by hand, wrist, and forearm.

While one arm is moving up and out of the water, the other arm should be pulling down and back so that it passes near the middle of your body and extends to your hip. During that pull, keep your fingers together, but relaxed. This completes half a cycle of stroking. Continue stroking by extending and pulling with the opposite arm to complete a full cycle. Breathe every other stroke, or each time the same arm is back towards the hip.

Nearly all of the forward motion is supplied by the pull, but a proper kick also helps propel you through the water. It also keeps your feet near the surface of the water, which saves you some work. If you didn't kick, your legs would sink and you would have to drag them through the water. Use what swimmers call the flutter kick. It resembles a short and snappy walking step. The movement for the flutter begins at the hips and should include 4 to 6 kicks for every cycle of your arm stroking.

*Breaststroke swimming*: The breaststroke combines a frog kick with an arm stroke where both arms pull simultaneously. Lie in the water face down with your arms straight out before you, legs extended back, and water level at your forehead. Push your arms out away from your body under the water until they're extended sideways and about even with your chest. At the same time, bring your legs up by bending at the knees.

To complete the arm stroke, draw your hands together near your chest and follow by pushing them in front of you again, as when you started. As your hands come together, straighten your legs to the sides (outward) and then snap them together to complete their cycle. Develop timing between the leg and arm movements so that your legs snap together as your arms straighten in front of you.

Inhale with each cycle during the breaststroke by lifting your chin out of the water during the arm stroke (the pull). Keep your mouth facing straight ahead. Exhale in the water as your arms come together.

## How Much to Swim

It's never easy to tell anyone how much or how fast to swim because of the danger of overdoing the activity in the water and then not getting out safely to rest. Nevertheless, as with running, you need at least 15 minutes of swimming to properly exercise your circulatory and respiratory systems (slightly less for pre-teen swimmers). But, with safety in mind, don't be reluctant to mix your swimming time with several rest periods. *Do not overdo it in the water!* If you can barely swim two laps nonstop in the pool (a lap is from one side of the pool to the other), then swim only one lap at a time, resting long enough in between laps to regain your strength. As you work out regularly, you'll find less and less need for rest periods.

Speed is not so important in aerobic swimming. You'll find, however, that when your stamina and technique improve and you're able to swim several laps nonstop, your speed will also increase. A goal to shoot for is to swim about 100 yards (90 metres) in less than 2 minutes (or 100 metres in less than $2\frac{1}{4}$ minutes). If you can manage to do 700 yards (630 metres) nonstop, then you know you've had a good workout.

# Wheeling Your Way into Condition

Bicycling has come a long way since an Englishman named James Moore won the first recorded bike race in 1868. Cyclist Moore rode to victory in a 2-kilometre ($1\frac{1}{4}$-mile) race in Paris, France, on a *velocipede*, a chainless vehicle with the pedals attached directly to the front wheel. Today, riders travel long distances on sturdy, light-weight, 10-speed bicycles. Some people have even ridden coast to coast across the United States, averaging nearly 100 miles (160 kilometres) a day. According to the *Guinness Book of World Records*, Paul Cornish, age 25, rode from San Francisco to New York in only 13 days! The youngest person to ride across the United States is Becky Gorton, age 11. She started from Olympia, Washington, on June 6, 1973 and arrived in Boston, Massachusetts on July 22, 1973.

Riding a bike is more than an unpolluting and inexpensive means of travel. It's also a good way to get aerobic exercise—possibly one you can fit into your daily schedule.

## How to Get into Cycling

One of the first decisions to make when planning an aerobic cycling course is deciding what kind of bike to ride. If your main interest is in fitness, not travel or racing, any bike in good working order will do. A banana-seated, one-speed bike with thick tires can do as well as a thin-tired, 10-speed, light-weight racing bike with curved handlebars. In fact, one-speed bikes are better as exercise machines because they're somewhat harder to pedal. Their disadvantage, however, is that their heavier weight and single gear make them too difficult to ride on long trips or bike tours.

Your attire for bicycling will depend on the weather. In hot weather, a short-sleeved shirt and shorts are fine. When it's cold, wear a warm jacket or a couple of sweat shirts, and heavy pants. You can always bring extra clothes with you, either in a backpack or in a nylon bag attached to the back of your seat or to the handle-bars. For foot protection, a good pair of running shoes and thick socks are needed.

Depending on how your bike is designed, you may have trouble with your pants legs catching in the chain and sprocket. This is not only annoying, but can also soil your clothes. To avoid this problem, use the metal clips or nylon straps that bike shops sell to place around your ankles for holding your pants snugly against your legs.

One of the most important items you can buy is a helmet. As careful a rider as you may be, bicycle accidents do happen and you certainly want to prevent a head injury. Many light-weight, strong helmets are available in bicycle and sporting-goods shops. If you ride on long tours in the bright sunshine, particularly in the summer or at high altitudes where the sun is intense, use a skin lotion or suntan oil. A sunburn over your legs, face and arms can make you wish you hadn't gone.

With your bicycle and gear ready, your next decision is to decide where to ride during your regular workouts. First, look for special bike trails or paths near your home. These are paved roads reserved for bicycles only—no cars allowed—and are the safest routes for riding. After that, choose streets and roads that have little traffic. Possibly you can use the route to your school or office, and that way combine aerobics with transportation. But by all means, stay off streets with steady flows of cars and trucks.

Many areas have cycling clubs. You may want to join one for the courses they offer in bike safety and repair, and for providing a great opportunity to meet other people interested in cycling. Many of these organizations have weekly group-rides around local areas as well as longer bike tours and overnight trips to near-by scenic places.

Bike riding is fun, excellent exercise, and an inexpensive way to get from place to place. But it can also be dangerous if you get careless. Almost half a million cyclists receive hospital treatment for injuries, and over 1,000 people are killed in bicycle accidents every year in the United States alone.

Here are some safety tips to keep in mind. Obey all traffic regulations (stop at stop signs and red lights, etc.). Slow down at major intersections, even if you have the right of way. Always ride on the right side of the road (left in some countries), *with* the traffic. At intersections with busy streets, stop and walk your bike across. When riding with another biker, ride single file. As you ride down a street lined with parked cars, be wary of any with people in them—someone may suddenly open the door on the driver's side in front of you and cause you to crash into it.

You must also watch out for road hazards. Do not ride on streets slippery with snow and ice. Be careful of drainage grates, too. Some are designed in a way that will catch your wheel as you ride over them. Finally, always wear a helmet. By taking the precautions outlined above, you may never experience an accident. But if you do, the helmet might save your life.

A number of magazines give useful tips on cycling, trip planning, bike repair and safety. Some of these are: *Bike World, Canadian Cyclist*; in England, *International Cycle Sport* and *Cycling* ; and in Australia, *Cycle Australia*.

## How to Ride Properly

The first step towards efficient cycling is to adjust the seat, or saddle, as cyclists call bicycle seats. Because your legs do nearly all the work, they must be at just the right distance from the pedals. If they're too close, your knees will be too high to allow you to push down with full leg power. On the other hand, if you must stretch to reach the pedals, you won't have full power then either. The ideal seat height is the one that allows you to put your foot on a pedal in its lowest position while allowing your leg to bend slightly at the knee.

The seat has two other adjustments. One is for tilting the seat to

**Cycling is fun and a good aerobic exercise besides.**

whatever angle feels comfortable. Another adjustment is for moving the saddle towards the handlebars or away from them. The seat should be in a position so you don't have to reach uncomfortably to grab the handlebars, but not so close that you're practically on top of them. You should be able to place your elbow on the front of the saddle and touch your fingertips to the back of the handlebars. Your handlebars should be at about the same height as the top of your saddle.

As you ride, keep the balls of your feet on the pedals. This permits your calf muscles to deliver optimum power. Leaning forward allows you to bear down harder on the pedals and also reduces resistance from the wind. Keep your head up, however, so you can see where you're going.

## How Much to Ride

Remember that most of the benefits of aerobic exercises come from working your heart and lungs more than you normally do. Other benefits come from building strength in the leg muscles. But because bicycles give you a mechanical advantage over running and swimming, you must exercise longer to gain the full benefits. Ride for at least 20 minutes (slightly less for pre-teen riders), travelling about one mile (1.6 kilometres) in 3 to 5 minutes. That's about 12 to 20 miles (20 to 30 kilometres) per hour. If you ride slower than this, you'll have to ride for a longer time before getting a thorough workout.

As long as you end up at the same elevation as you started at, hills don't affect your workout. Although you can pedal downhill with ease, you'll have to pedal hard uphill to maintain an average pace of 12 to 20 miles (20 to 30 kilometres) per hour.

Riding for at least 20 minutes at 12 to 20 miles (20 to 30 kilometres) per hour means you cover a distance of 4 to 6 miles (7 to 10 kilometres). Bike as far as you want, so long as you don't push yourself beyond your limits and have trouble returning home.

# Jumping into Shape

Almost everyone has jumped rope at one time or another. Most people, however, don't think of it as a way to get into shape. But boxers like Muhammad Ali and Ken Norton have long recognized that rope jumping has a lot to offer: it improves coordination and agility, and is also a good aerobic exercise. Jumping rope even builds strength in the thighs and calves. Some people have built up outstanding endurance through rope jumping. Rabbi Barry Silberg of Milwaukee, Wisconsin, demonstrated this when he jumped 43,473 times without a break on June 22, 1975. It took the Rabbi 5 hours to set this world's record.

Jumping rope appeals to many people. One feature they like is that it doesn't require leaving the house (provided the ceilings in

**Swimming is an excellent aerobic exercise.**

the house are high enough for jumping). This saves time and keeps them out of the cold, heat, rain, and snow.

## How to Get into Rope Jumping

The only piece of equipment you absolutely need is a rope. Sporting-goods shops carry first-class jump ropes with swivel handles. You can make your own, however, out of a piece of clothesline rope. Whatever rope you use, it should be heavy enough to allow turning it easily. If it's too light in weight, you'll use up too much energy just making it turn.

The length of the rope is also important. A rope that's too short will force you to bend over and perhaps throw you off balance. If it's too long, it will slap against the floor in front of you and possibly just stop there. To determine the correct length, stand on the rope and hold up the ends. They should reach about up to your arm pits.

Dress comfortably for jumping; wear clothes that don't bind. If you exercise outside, wear clothing appropriate for the weather. Shoes with good arch supports and padding are important, plus thick socks. Your feet do a lot of work when you jump rope for 20 minutes and they deserve some special attention.

## How to Jump Properly

There is more than one way to skip rope. The simplest is to jump once for each turn of the rope. Another way is to add an extra skip as the rope is making the trip around again. This method gives you more exercise, develops better timing, and strengthens your legs more.

A third way is to bounce on only one foot at a time. You can use the same foot for a period of time or alternate feet each time the rope comes around. Whichever methods you choose should depend on what feels most comfortable. Most people find it enjoyable to continuously switch jumping styles.

You should stand erect while jumping, with your head up and eyes looking straight ahead. You may lose your timing if you look at the rope or at your feet. Start with the rope behind you and bring it up and around, over your head. As it approaches your feet, time your jump so that the rope glides under them. Land on the balls of your feet and provide the power for the jump from your calves and ankles, and not from your knees and thighs.

## How Much to Jump

Since you must get your heart beating faster than it normally does, turn the rope around quite fast—75 to 100 times per minute. Exactly how fast depends partly on how long you want to work out on a particular day. If you would like a short, fast workout, make the rope move around 100 times or more a minute. A longer, more leisurely workout needs only about 75 jumps per minute.

Your goal should be to jump rope for about 15 minutes (slightly less for pre-teen jumpers), preferably 20 minutes. Because the exercise does not make your heart beat as fast as running or swimming, you should jump rope for a longer period of time.

## Hints for Any Aerobic Exercise

Whether you run, swim, cycle, or jump rope for your aerobic exercise, there are two general rules to follow: take time to warm up before exercising and to cool down afterwards. Following both rules helps prevent injuries and soreness, and accommodates the changes needed in blood circulation and distribution.

Your warm-up comes in two parts. The most important is stretching your muscles before your workout. Loosening up will reduce or prevent soreness and strains by preparing the muscles for the hard work you're about to undertake. Before you run, swim, cycle, or jump rope, go through a 5- to 10-minute stretching routine that includes movements such as twisting, toe touches and leg stretches. Read the suggestions and instructions for stretching in Chapter 2. Whichever group of loosening movements you choose, be sure that it includes stretching of the muscles directly involved in your particular workout.

The other part of your warm-up comes as you begin your aerobic workout. At each session, start your aerobic exercise at an easy pace. Don't push your body before it's ready to perform at its best. Like stretching, increasing your pace gradually reduces the chances of muscle soreness and injuries. Believe it or not, most distance runners prepare for a race by jogging for about 10 minutes, and swimmers will spend 15 to 30 minutes doing laps before a meet. Competitors never feel ready to race all out until they've gotten all the kinks out and muscles warmed up.

After your hard exercise, *do not* just sit down immediately. Cool down gradually by walking (or swimming or cycling slowly). It's

## Running Regimens

Run for the indicated number of minutes, trying to maintain a pace faster than 9 minutes per mile (5½ minutes per kilometre).

### Schedule

|  | Minutes | | | |
|---|---|---|---|---|
| days per week | preteens 9-12 years | early teens 13-15 years | late teens 16-19 years | post-teens |
| 3 | 12 | 14 | 16 | 16 |
| 4 | 10 | 12 | 14 | 14 |
| 5 | 8 | 10 | 12 | 12 |

## Swimming Regimens

Swim for the indicated number of minutes, trying to maintain a pace faster than 2 minutes per 100 yards (2¼ minutes per 100 metres).

### Schedule

|  | Minutes | | | |
|---|---|---|---|---|
| days per week | preteens 9-12 years | early teens 13-15 years | late teens 16-19 years | post-teens |
| 3 | 16 | 18 | 20 | 20 |
| 4 | 14 | 16 | 18 | 18 |
| 5 | 12 | 14 | 16 | 16 |

also a good idea to include a few more stretching exercises during your cool-down period. Devote several minutes to cooling off—it will help you to avoid muscle cramps, soreness, and to rid your muscles of waste products.

Your entire aerobics workout, including warm-up, cool-down, and shower, should not take longer than one hour.

## Key Points for Successful Aerobics

■ Before any workout, warm up thoroughly by stretching your muscles (see Chapter 2 for details on stretching exercises).

■ Wear clothing that's both comfortable and suitable for the weather. When running in cold weather, wear layers of clothing that you can take off as you become warmer during the run.

■ When running or jumping rope, wear a good pair of running shoes, both for comfort and to prevent injuries to your feet and legs.

■ Use proper form in running, swimming, biking, or jumping rope to help prevent injuries and to get the most benefit from your aerobics.

■ *Do not* overexert yourself by trying to accomplish too much at one time. Rest when necessary, especially when aerobics is new to you.

■ Remember the safety rules. Avoid running on streets heavy with traffic. Don't swim without a buddy or out of sight and reach of a lifeguard. Obey traffic regulations when cycling.

■ Wait at least one hour after eating a meal before working out.

■ Cool down gradually after a workout. Don't finish running, for example, and drop down into a chair. Walk around for several minutes afterwards.

## Cycling Regimens

Cycle for the indicated number of minutes, trying to maintain a pace faster than 5 minutes per mile (3 minutes per kilometre).

**Minutes**

| Schedule days per week | preteens 9-12 years | early teens 13-15 years | late teens 16-19 years | post-teens |
|---|---|---|---|---|
| 3 | 16 | 22 | 28 | 28 |
| 4 | 14 | 19 | 24 | 24 |
| 5 | 12 | 15 | 20 | 20 |

## Rope-Jumping Regimens

Jump rope for the indicated number of minutes for your age group, trying to maintain a pace of at least 75 jumps per minute.

**Minutes**

| Schedule days per week | preteens 9-12 years | early teens 13-15 years | late teens 16-19 years | post-teens |
|---|---|---|---|---|
| 3 | 14 | 18 | 22 | 22 |
| 4 | 12 | 16 | 20 | 20 |
| 5 | 10 | 14 | 18 | 18 |

# Your Aerobics Program for Growing Strong

There's such a variety of aerobic exercises that you may actually have trouble deciding which one to begin with. It can be especially tough to decide if you're enthusiastic about all forms of physical activity that lead to good health, stamina, and strength, and are interested in trying each one to see which brings the best results.

All the aerobics discussed here are excellent for developing stamina and strength, so choose one that has the most appeal and will fit best into your schedule for school and other weekly activities. And take into account, too, the environment around you—the weather, the season, the availability of a pool and good running and biking trails. Most importantly, however, select at least one aerobic exercise and begin your program—*now*.

For any activity you choose, you must know how often to work at it. As we pointed out earlier, the amount of time you put into an aerobic exercise has a lot to do with the benefit you receive in return. The general rule for aerobics is to work out at least 3 days a week. You might, for example, run on Mondays, Wednesdays, and Fridays, leaving Tuesdays, Thursdays, and the weekends for rest or for strength-building exercises (Chapters 4 and 5). If you choose not to combine aerobics with strength-building exercises, you may want to run up to 5 days a week. This could be each weekday, saving the weekends for 2 days of rest. The times of day that you work out is not so important, but try to remain consistent from session to session. If you go down to the pool in the early evening on Monday, for example, try to go at the same times Wednesday and Friday as well.

Remember that it takes a certain amount of time for each exercise to work your heart and lungs enough to achieve improvements in endurance and all-round physical condition. In general, about 15 minutes is needed—but a little less time each session is adequate for the pre-teen ages. Also, when you're active at aerobics up to 5 times a week, you need less workout time each session than for a 3-day-a-week schedule. That is, the amount of time you put in over a week's period is also important, so the fewer workout days you have in one week, the longer the workout time you need each session.

The recommended times are presented in the regimens. Work towards these goals, and when you've reached them, either stay with those times or challenge yourself by increasing them another 5 or 10 minutes. Note, however, that pre-teens should not try to out-do an adult at long endurance times.

After you've achieved a regular pace at running, swimming, or biking, and have developed endurance for the recommended times, you may then want to measure your distances against your times. Do this by running around a track or by swimming measured lengths of a pool.

Be sure to rest when you need to, especially when you're just beginning. Short rest periods are necessary while your body is becoming accustomed to an aerobics program. When running or jumping rope, take a walking break. For swimming, stay near the edge of the pool or where you can stand up at any time. And when cycling, slow down to a gentle pedal or coast along for a while.

Each aerobic regimen assumes you do not do the others. But don't hesitate to combine two or more different types. For example, running two days a week and swimming two days is an effective combination. For many people, a variety in the types of workouts makes their fitness training more exciting and easier to stay with. It's a good idea, however, to do one particular exercise at least twice a week to assure that you gain some strength in the muscles it involves.

## Questions and Answers

*I plan to work as a lifeguard this summer. Although I run 2 miles (3.2 kilometres) 4 times a week, I'd like to substitute swimming. Will I have any problems in making this change?*

The only difficulty you might have is sore muscles as you start your swimming regimen. Your heart and lungs are ready for anything, but you will use all the muscles in your upper body, which you do not do in running.

*I ride my bike about a mile and a half (2.5 kilometres) to and from school each day. Isn't that enough exercise?*

No, it isn't, because you don't do the exercise for a long enough time to get your body to respond to the exercise. If you can, leave early and ride an extra couple of miles, perhaps by taking a longer route.

*I have a friend on the track team. He says that you must run fast to get in good shape. Can't you get into shape by running slowly for a longer distance?*

Of course you can. You can even get into shape by walking briskly. If you run fast and you only do it for 3 or 4 minutes, it doesn't do you much good.

*I use weights 3 times a week, eat a balanced diet, and don't smoke. Why should I do an aerobic exercise? Isn't the weight training enough?*

No. Weight training builds up your muscles, but each set of exercises doesn't last long enough to strengthen your heart and lungs. In fact, aerobic exercise is even more important for a weightlifter because the added muscles must be supplied with blood, which, of course, must be pumped by the heart.

*You warned against pushing ourselves too hard. How can I tell if I've gone beyond my limits?*

If you push yourself too hard, you'll feel ill while working out. Your head might ache, you could feel nauseated and your muscles might cramp. If any of these symptoms appear every time you work out, you will feel tired *all* the time, just the opposite of how a physically-fit person should feel. If you start to feel poorly like this, take a few days off. When you resume your workouts, exercise less vigorously.

*A friend of mine smokes half a pack of cigarettes a day, but he also runs a mile and a half (2.5 kilometres) 5 days a week. He says the running makes up for the smoking. Does it?*

No, it does not make up for smoking. Your friend may be healthier than a nonrunning smoker, but he is also a lot worse off than a nonsmoking runner. Smoking produces the opposite effects that aerobic exercise does.

*What about the adults who run 5 or 10 miles (8 or 16 kilometres) a day? Is that much running necessary for an adult to stay in good shape?*

No, it's not necessary, but the people who run that far enjoy doing it, and many enter long-distance races to test their capabilities. For most adults, however, 2 miles (3.2 kilometres) a day 3 times a week is adequate.

## Chapter 4

# BUILDING MUSCLE THROUGH SIMPLE EXERCISE

Strength is built through resistance. When the movements of muscles are resisted, extra strength is needed to overcome the outside forces. The more often muscles struggle to overcome resistance, the stronger they become.

Long before weightlifting became the popular way to offer resistance to muscles, simple exercises were the most convenient methods of building strength. In these movements, such as push-ups and pull-ups, your own bodyweight acts as the resistance, and today, many people still use these body-resistance exercises as great strength builders. You can build up your arms and shoulders by pulling or pushing the weight of your body (doing pull-ups or push-ups), or you can develop stronger legs by using your body to resist the movements of your legs (doing squats).

The nice features about such exercises are that they require no special equipment (except, perhaps, for a pull-up bar) and they can be done almost anywhere at any time. Instead of using equipment such as weights, you lift or push yourself as a weight. Your increase in strength comes from doing several repetitions of the same exercise.

The number of repetitions (and sets) you do for your age is one of the keys to building strength. And you can expect the strength to come rather quickly by doing the workouts prescribed here.

**Keep your body straight when doing push-ups.**
**Gently touch your chin to the floor.**

This holds for both boys and girls—either can work up to equal repetitions of these exercises and achieve equal strength.

But simple exercise is by no means the end to strength development. Although an important part of growing strong, exercise has its limits, too. The reason is that you can't increase the weight of the resistance (your body), and therefore you eventually reach a point where the exercise is no longer effective for increasing muscular strength. (This is why weightlifting—Chapter 5—is the king of strength-building methods.) On the other hand, simple exercises are the best way to set the solid groundwork for strength—especially for young people.

All it takes is a 3-day-a-week program. By working regularly at these exercises, you'll be assured of achieving and maintaining good muscular development. We describe more exercises than you need to do on a regular basis, but you can pick out the ones you like best or switch from one to another from time to time. Just be sure that you regularly work all of your major muscle groups.

You'll notice that some of the exercises are good for stretching as well as strength building—there's sometimes a fine dividing line between movements that stretch and those that strengthen. However, one difference to remember about strength-building exercises is the need to control your breathing during the movements: inhale during the easier part of an exercise and exhale while in the strenuous movement.

As for attire, dress in a warm-up suit or in shorts and a T-shirt or sweat shirt. And be sure to *remain* warm while working out. Wear a comfortable pair of running shoes.

## Strengthening Your Chest, Arms, and Shoulders
### Push-Ups

The push-up is the most basic exercise for adding strength to your triceps and pecs. Lie face down with your hands on the floor, spacing them slightly wider than your shoulders. Your fingers should be pointing forward. Inhale, and then push yourself off the floor until your arms are fully extended. Exhale throughout the push and be certain to keep your body straight and rigid. Then slowly lower yourself, resisting gravity with your arms, keeping your form, and inhaling along the way down. Simply touch your chest or chin lightly to the floor and push up again.

For more advanced push-ups, place your hands on blocks (or books) about 1 inch (2.5 cm) thick. This way, you have slightly farther to go to touch your chin to the floor. Push-ups from blocks really work your chest well.

If you find regular push-ups becoming easy after a while, then

**Hang straight from the pull-up (chinning) bar before starting.**

**Be sure your chin goes over the bar. You can also use the reverse grip for your pull-ups.**

try this more difficult version. Lie on the floor as usual, but when you push up, use enough upward spring so that you lift off the floor and have time to clap your hands together before you come down. Don't expect to be able to do as many reps as you were doing for regular push-ups.

## Pull-Ups

Pull-ups (sometimes called chin-ups) strengthen your biceps, forearms, and deltoids. To do this exercise, however, you need a bar parallel to the ground and higher than you. A pull-up bar can be built in your backyard, or you can use one in a school playground. You may also find the horizontal supports of a backyard swing set handy for pull-ups. Even a sturdy tree limb can do the trick.

Grab the bar, palms facing you, and hang from it. Your hands should be about in line with your shoulders. Inhale first, and then pull yourself up, exhaling along the way, until your chin is above the bar. When you lower yourself, be sure to come down slowly, offering resistance, and inhale on the way down. When you reach your lowest hanging point, your elbows should be straight. Keep your legs straight and your body firm throughout the entire pull-up movement.

It's slightly more difficult to do pull-ups with your palms facing away from you, a reverse grip. Aside from the position of your hands, the reverse grip pull-up is done in the same fashion as the other pull-up. This method does, however, work the deltoids more and the biceps less, and it emphasizes different forearm muscles. For the most thorough arm and shoulder development, do both forward and reverse grip pull-ups.

## The Way to Strong Abdominal Muscles

### Sit-Ups

Strong muscles in the stomach region are important whether you play sports, or need strength to rearrange the furniture in your room, or whether you just want to look good. Sit-ups are one of the best ways to develop the abdominal area.

The basic technique for sit-ups is to lie on your back with your legs straight and together and with your hands clasped behind your head or neck. Then, while keeping your legs straight, pull yourself up using only your stomach muscles. To keep your legs down, you may need to tuck your toes beneath a piece of furniture, like a couch, or use a partner to hold your ankles. Don't stop when you reach a sitting-up position, but continue moving towards your knees, always keeping your legs straight. Stop when you feel a strong tugging on your hamstrings and hold for a second. As you lie back down, resist the motion with your abs so you lower yourself to the floor gradually rather than flopping back. Continue with another sit-up.

**(Top) The lying-down position for sit-ups. (Middle) Starting up. (Bottom) Lean over fully to complete the sit-up.**

Since the straight-legged sit-up uses muscles other than just the abdominals, you may want to isolate your stomach area better by doing sit-ups with your knees bent. These are done by lying on the floor with your knees bent and your hands behind your head or neck. Sit up, curling as you rise, and touch your elbows to your knees. Gradually lower yourself and repeat the bent-knee sit-up.

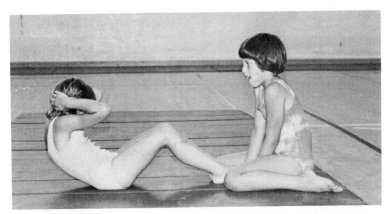

**When doing the bent-knee sit-up, have your feet firmly held. Use your stomach muscles to curl up towards your knees.**

For a greater challenge, try either "V" sit-ups or tuck-ups. To do the "V" sit-up, lie on your back with your legs straight and hands at your sides. Now sit up, but lift your legs at the same time, keeping them straight. Your arms should stay level with the floor and your body should form a "V." Lie flat again and repeat. Tuck-ups are similar, except you bend your legs as you sit up and bring your knees to your chest.

### Leg Raises

Leg raises are another way to make your abdominal muscles strong, especially in the lower stomach region. Instead of lifting your upper body off the floor as you do in sit-ups, you lift your legs. Lie on your back, legs straight, and with your hands at your sides, palms down. Slowly lift your legs off the floor without bending at the knees. Lift your legs until they're pointing up towards the ceiling. Then lower them slowly to the floor.

A more difficult version of leg raises is to do them while hanging from a bar. This exercise is a must for gymnasts, as it offers a workout to arm, shoulder, and lower back muscles in addition to

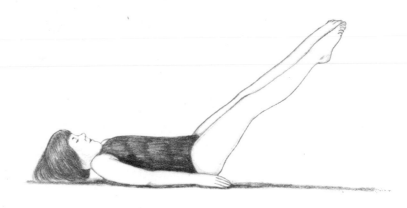

**Begin leg raises by lying flat. Keep your back flat and raise your legs.**

the abdominals. Start by hanging from a bar, then begin to lift your legs, keeping them straight throughout the movement. Stop when your legs are level with the ground, and then lower them slowly. *Do not* swing your legs during this exercise. Just lift and lower them using your abdominal muscles. A goal to shoot for is to do a leg raise where you bring your feet completely up to the bar.

Leg raises while hanging are difficult and it's possible to strain yourself by trying them before your muscles are ready. Advance to this exercise only when you find two sets of sit-ups and leg raises on the floor to be quite easy for you.

## Developing Strong Back and Leg Muscles

### Extensions

The back muscles are not easy to strengthen by exercise, but extensions work quite well. Lie on your stomach with your body fully extended, legs straight, and arms outstretched above your head. Keeping your arms and legs straight, use your back muscles to lift your arms, head, chest and legs, leaving only your stomach on the floor. This is a tough one, so it may not be

Start the hanging leg raise from a bar as you would pull-ups.
Bring your legs up and level to the ground. With a really strong
abdomen, you can bring your feet up to the bar.

comfortable at first. When you've stretched into an arch, or
"rocking horse" position, as well as you can, hold the position
for a few seconds, then relax.

Extensions will give your back a workout.

Extensions are difficult. If you can't get your body off the floor completely, try just half of the exercise—lift only your arms and chest, letting your legs remain on the floor. Hold for up to 5 seconds and then relax. Then try lifting your legs up, leaving your chest and arms on the floor. After a few weeks of these upper- and lower-body lifts, you'll probably be able to do the complete extension.

## Squats

You can't consider yourself in good shape if you don't have strong leg muscles. Running and cycling are two ways to produce strong legs, but a more direct way to powerful legs is to do squats, or deep knee bends. Stand up straight with hands on your hips. Then, keeping your back straight to encourage good posture, squat down by bending your knees. Stand up again and repeat.

Your feet can sit flat on the floor, or you can stand on the balls of your feet. With your feet flat, descend only until your thighs are level with the floor. If you go deeper, you may bounce and put a

**Begin a squat thrust by squatting down with your palms on the floor. Kick out to the push-up position. Bring your legs in again, and stand up.**

strain on your knees. *Avoid this because it could lead to knee problems*. Squatting on the balls of your feet will bring your calf muscles into play and probably make it easier for you to balance as well. Again, *do not bounce on your knees*. In either stance, breathing for squatting should follow the pattern of inhaling before you squat and then exhaling through the entire movement.

Squats are easy enough that you have to do quite a number of them to develop your leg muscles. A more taxing variation of the exercise is squat jumps. These are started in the same fashion as squats, but you then spring up from the squat position (without bouncing on your knees). The jump flexes your muscles much more than does a slow rise.

You can also combine a leg exercise with an upper body exercise by doing squat thrusts. Stand erect with hands on hips, as for squats. Now, squat down on the balls of your feet and place your palms on the floor. Immediately thrust your feet backward so you end up in the push-up position with your arms straight. Quickly return to the squatted position, stand up, and repeat. Besides helping develop muscles, a set of fast-moving squat thrusts will put your respiratory and circulatory systems to work as well.

## Strength Builders That Need Special Equipment

### Dips

Dips are performed using parallel bars and they resemble push-ups, but your body remains vertical rather than horizontal. Like push-ups, dips will strengthen your triceps, deltoids, and pecs.

Many gyms have short parallel bars mounted on walls for doing dips. Support yourself between the parallel bars with arms straight and your feet hanging free. Most of the burden at this point is resting on your shoulders. Slowly lower yourself, bending at the elbows. Dip low enough so that your shoulders get as close to your hands as possible. Using triceps power, lift yourself up again until you are in the straight-arm starting position. Dips are decidedly hard to do, so you might try lowering yourself only half-way at first. It may also help to have a bench nearby to use for getting into the starting position and for dismounting.

### Rope or Pole Climb

If you like *Tarzan* movies, you'll enjoy the rope climb. Many gyms have thick ropes (or tall climbing poles) secured to the ceiling. An excellent way to develop strong arm and shoulder muscles is to climb up the rope, hand over hand. While climbing, wrap your feet around the rope to assist the pull. As you get stronger, try the climb without using your feet. A word of caution: gym ropes are usually attached to a ceiling 20 or more feet (6 metres or more) high—a long distance to fall. *Do not* go all the way up until you're confident that you can make it both up and down. And always be sure that there's a thick mat on the floor beneath the rope. It's wise to have a physical education instructor show you how to do the rope climb and remind you of the safety tips.

## Key Points for Successful Strength-Building Exercises

■ Always stretch before attempting strength-building exercises (see Chapter 2).

■ Dress so that you keep warm and comfortable.

■ Maintain proper form and style during each exercise. You get more out of doing an exercise if you do it as it should be done, rather than in a hurried manner using poor form and incorrect style.

■ *Do not* work out immediately after eating a meal. Wait at least one hour.

- Control your breathing. Inhale on the easier part of the movement, exhale when you really put your muscles to work. For example, exhale while pulling yourself up to a bar, and inhale as you lower yourself.

- When doing squats, have respect for your knees. *Do not* bounce on them.

- Remember safety and use good sense when it comes to hanging from bars and climbing ropes.

- Don't neglect exercising any parts of your body. You need strong arm, shoulder, chest, back, abdomen and leg muscles—all-around strength.

## Your Exercise Regimen for Growing Strong

Working out to build strength through exercise should be done on a 3-day-a-week schedule. For convenience, most people prefer a Monday-Wednesday-Friday schedule, taking the weekends off. You can, however, work out any 3-day sequence that best fits your schedule of other activities, just as long as you're consistent and rest once a week for two days straight. Those rest days between workouts are necessary to allow your body to fully recover—it's during those times when much of your muscular development and strength increase take place.

Approach each exercise set by aiming for the maximum number of repetitions recommended in the regimen for your age group. The suggested numbers may seem high, but those are your goals to shoot for.

After each set, rest one to two minutes before doing another. Usually your second and third sets will be lower in reps than the first because some of your strength will be temporarily used up from the first set. However, rather than resting between sets, you could switch to a set of an exercise that doesn't directly use the same muscles. In other words, alternate sets of different exercises. You might, for instance, mix push-ups with sit-ups.

Each workout should be rather short. A session lasting 30 minutes is usually plenty of time for working all of your major body parts. (This includes adequate resting time between sets.)

The repetitions suggested for each exercise and age are enough to provide you with good strength. In other words, there's no need to attempt a set of 100 push-ups or 50 pull-ups, unless you're trying to establish some new contest record. Doing an unusually high number of reps builds up endurance, but doesn't necessarily increase strength that much more.

The number of sets and reps and the 3-day-a-week regimen are prescribed as though the exercises are the only strength-building activities you'll do for growing up strong. If this is the case, each workout should contain at least one exercise from each of the 5 groups shown on page 83. With access to parallel bars or a rope, you can occasionally add sets of dips and a rope climb, too.

If you later combine your exercises with aerobic activities (running, jumping, swimming, biking—see Chapter 3), then you may wish to cut this regimen back to 2 days a week. If you choose to emphasize weightlifting (Chapter 5), many of these exercises will be replaced by exercises using weights.

## Questions and Answers

*I can do the exercise regimen in less than 20 minutes. Is that really all I have to do to be physically fit?*

That's all you need for well-toned and strong muscles, but don't forget to run, swim, or cycle to produce strong heart and lungs, and to increase your stamina. For really greater strength development, you'll have to lift weights, provided that you are at least in your teens.

*I do pull-ups and push-ups every day, but I find that I can't do as many some days as others. What's the cause of that?*

Everybody has off days once in a while when their strength is just not up to its best. If your problem isn't just an occasional off day, then maybe you're overtraining—doing too much without enough rest days in between workout days.

*I hate to admit it, but I can't even do one pull-up. How can I increase my strength if I can't even do that?*

Pull up as far as you can, then slowly lower yourself back down. Do as many of these "half pull-ups" as possible, always giving it all you have. The resistance on the way down will help to increase your strength and in a short time you should be doing one perfect pull-up. Another way to build up your number of reps is to have an assistant give you a slight boost when you reach your sticking point.

*I'm 14 years old and can do all the sets and reps suggested for an older teenager. I hope there's nothing wrong with me working on an advanced regimen.*

Not at all. There are always exceptions when it comes to physical fitness—and you seem to be exceptionally strong and well developed for one your age. This is often the case for young gymnasts.

*Is there anything wrong with doing several different exercises for the same muscle group during one workout period? Say, could I do several types of sit-ups and leg raises in one day?*

This is fine if you want to really concentrate on developing a particular area over others. For example, many boys do large numbers of pull-ups trying to build their arms and shoulders. You can do this as long as you don't overtrain—at which time you'll begin to actually notice decreases in your strength.

## Warming Up

*For these strength-building exercises* . . . . . . . *do these★ stretching movements:*

push-ups, pull-ups, dips, and rope climb
- shoulder rotations—10 reps each arm, each direction
- side bends—5-10 reps on each side
- toe touches (with back bends)—10 reps

sit-ups and leg raises
- twisting—5 reps
- bridges—3-5 reps

extensions
- kickovers—5 reps
- bridges—3-5 reps
- twisting—5 reps
- side bends—5-10 reps on each side
- toe touches (with back bends)—10 reps

squats and squat thrusts
- toe touches (with back bends)—10 reps
- leg stretches—5 reps each leg
- lunges—5 reps each leg

★No more than two movements are needed to prepare for each strength-building exercise; see Chapter 2 for details of stretching movements.

# Working out

*Select at least one exercise from each group (per workout)**

| | Pre-teens 9–12 years | Early teens 13–15 years | Late teens 16–19 years | Post-teens |
|---|---|---|---|---|
| | *sets/reps* | *sets/reps* | *sets/reps* | *sets/reps* |
| I Push-ups | 3/8–10 | 3/12–14 | 3/15–20 | 2/20–25 |
| II Pull-ups | | | | |
|   forward grip (for biceps) | 2/5–7 | 2/6–8 | 3/7–10 | 3/8–12 |
|   reverse grip (for deltoids) | 2/4–6 | 2/5–7 | 3/6–9 | 3/8–12 |
| III Sit-ups and leg raises | | | | |
|   straight-legged sit-ups | 1/40 | 1/50–60 | 2/50–60 | 2/50–75 |
|   bent-knee sit-ups | 1/40 | 1/50–60 | 2/50–60 | 2/50–75 |
|   "v" sit-ups | 1/40 | 1/50–60 | 2/50–60 | 2/50–75 |
|   tuck-ups | 1/40 | 1/50–60 | 2/50–60 | 2/50–75 |
|   leg raises, on floor | 2/15–20 | 2/20–25 | 2/20–25 | 2/20–25 |
|   leg raises, on bar | 1/3–5 | 2/3–5 | 2/5–7 | 3/5–7 |
| IV Extensions | 1/2–3 | 1/4–5 | 2/3–5 | 2/4–5 |
| V Squats | | | | |
|   normal | 2/15–20 | 2/20–25 | 3/20–25 | 3/20–25 |
|   jumps | 2/10–15 | 2/15–20 | 3/15–20 | 3/15–20 |
|   squat thrusts | 2/10–15 | 2/15–20 | 3/15–20 | 3/15–20 |
| Dips | 1/6–8 | 2/6–8 | 2/8–10 | 3/8–10 |
| Rope (or pole) climb (without using legs for assistance) | 1 climb to 10 feet (3 metres) | 1 climb to 15 feet (4½ metres) | 1 climb to 20 feet (6 metres) | 1 climb to 20 feet (6 metres) |

*The sets and reps are the goals to reach for in your age group.

## Chapter 5

# WEIGHTLIFTING—THE MASTERLINK TO STRENGTH

Weightlifting can develop tremendous strength. Few can argue that statement, but even fewer people have any idea of the kind of power that can be packed into muscles. As an example, consider that there are some small men who weigh 125 pounds (56 kg) and are able to press 225 pounds (100 kg) over their heads. Then there are larger men of 225 pounds (100 kg) who easily lift 600 pounds (275 kg) from the floor to their hips. And these are not even weightlifting records. Here are some world records: 330-pound (150-kg) Vasili Alexeev of the Soviet Union has pressed more than 500 pounds (225 kg) over his head, and the 185-pound (85-kg) Vince Anello of the United States has pulled over 700 pounds (315 kg) from the floor.

None of these weightlifting feats come easily for anybody, of course—they require years of training. But as examples, they illustrate that lifting weights while growing up will assure you of much better than average strength.

Women, too, are getting into weightlifting nowadays. Many have increased their strength to where they can lift 150 pounds (67 kg) or more. A number of women today are clearly stronger than men equal to them in size, and many are using their new strength to enter weightlifting contests with men. Women's interest in weightlifting has grown rapidly since it became well known that lifting will not create great muscle size in women.

But there's more to weightlifting than gaining power. Just like running, swimming, or any of the aerobics (Chapter 3), this activity does a lot to increase overall health and endurance. Plus, there is the bonus of weightlifting bringing out your best physical appearance: it helps trim away excess bodyweight and develop eye-appealing muscle proportions.

Some caution must be given, however, about including weightlifting in your regimen for growing strong. *You should be at least a teenager before you begin lifting weights.* This is not to say there is any danger in weightlifting. Rather, it is important that your muscle and bone structures have reached a certain level of development before expecting them to respond properly to exercise with weights.

As for safety, weightlifting offers far less danger than any contact sport. Common sense, of course, is important in any form of physical activity. You must have proper respect for the weights, just like the football player respects his opponent's ability to block hard, and just like skaters show regard for the slippery ice. This means that you must never attempt to lift a weight without some knowledge of how heavy it will be *for you*, and how much of an effort will be needed to lift it.

## How to Get into Lifting

Growing strong by weightlifting requires that you own a set of weights with enough bars and plates to construct a barbell and two dumbbells. The total weight to begin with should be approximately 100 pounds (45kg). You can buy a new set of weights at most sports equipment shops or you can order from companies that advertise in magazines. One money-saving way is to obtain used equipment. A good set of weights won't wear out and you can often find them for sale at low prices in the classified ad section of your newspaper or at garage sales.

**This assortment of weights and the special bench to use for bench pressing were purchased cheaply at garage sales.**

If you plan to lift weights at home, you may wish to consider using weight-plates that are vinyl-covered. Vinyl-covered plates are usually concrete discs covered with plastic. They are quiet to use, but are not as long-lasting or sturdy as iron plates.

Another piece of equipment you may want to purchase or construct is a rugged bench—preferably a bench with supports at one end to place a barbell. You'll find this equipment valuable for the lifting exercises that put strength in your pectoral muscles.

There are places other than home where you can begin weightlifting. Perhaps your school gymnasium has weights, or you may even find an outside gym where there are a number of other eager lifters to work out with. A buddy system can help you maintain a good attitude and make better progress at your lifting. On the other hand, an advantage to weightlifting at home is that you have the privacy and freedom to work out any time of day you choose. Whether working out at home or away, it's a good idea to have a partner to assist you with certain lifts.

Dress appropriately any time and place you work out. Keeping warm is important. In cool weather, wear a sweatshirt or a complete sweatsuit and make certain that your workout area is well heated. In warm weather, a T-shirt and shorts are enough clothing, but stay out of air currents and away from blasting air conditioners. Under any conditions be sure that your clothes don't confine your lifting movements. A good pair of running shoes is also important to wear while working out.

Weightlifting has its own special terms that you'll want to learn. Reps and sets are words commonly used and were defined in Chapter 4. The word *clean* has an unusual definition in weightlifting circles. To clean a weight is to bring it from the floor up to a position where you're standing upright and holding it at chest level. The proper way to clean is described in a following section.

*Spotters* are needed for some weightlifting exercises. A spotter is another lifter who carefully watches you for safety purposes while you perform a set. Most exercises don't require a spotter, particularly if you can easily and safely drop the weights if necessary. But for some lifts with a barbell, it's helpful to have a spotter standing by to take the barbell if you happen to go beyond your limit and cannot complete a movement. During a good workout, blood rushes to the muscles that suddenly need a large supply of oxygen. The term *pump* refers to this flooding of muscles with blood after doing a resistance exercise. Commonly, that "pumped-up" feeling lasts about an hour. Recently, the phrase "pumping iron" has become popular to apply to using weights (iron). You will quickly understand that expression after doing a few good sets of an arm exercise.

Most all special interests today have magazines devoted to them. Weightlifting has them too. Three popular ones found on newsstands are *Strength and Health, Muscular Development,* and *Iron Man.* All of these are bi-monthly publications. In Great

Britain, the weightlifting magazine is *Strength Athlete*, and in Australia, *Australian Weight Lifting Journal*.

## Lifting Weights the Right Way

There is certain basic information you need to know about any physical activity—for American football, you learn to grip the ball properly, for soccer, being able to dribble with a steady rhythm is a must. In weightlifting, knowing how to clean the weight is important. The reason for this is that several weightlifting movements call for you to get the bar from the floor up to your chest—to clean the weight. The right way to do a clean is as follows.

Place the bar horizontally on the floor before you and set your feet so that your shins are about 2 inches (5 cm) from the bar. Your heels should be about shoulder-width or somewhat closer, and your toes should point slightly outward.

Get set for the clean by reaching down to grasp the bar with an overhand (palms-down) grip, hands outside your legs and at about shoulder-width. Your arms should be straight and your shoulders should lean slightly out in front of the bar. Keep your buttocks as low as comfortably possible, and your back flat. Look ahead, not at the bar.

Begin the pull on the bar by driving with every muscle in your legs—the thighs, buttocks, and hips. Do not, however, raise your buttocks before the bar leaves the floor.

The bar should rise in a vertical path. As it passes your hips, you should be standing straight and extended up on the balls of your feet. Immediately move quickly to drop slightly below the bar by bending at the knees. At the same time, whip your wrists around so your palms face up and the bar is brought to your shoulders. The clean is complete when you stand up straight with the bar held at your upper chest. When it comes to placing weights back down on the floor, do it gently. Treat both your weights and your workout area so they last.

Begin the clean (above) with feet near the bar and back flat.

Drive up (right) with leg power . . . up on your toes.

Dip down slightly to get beneath the bar (below). Finish cleaning by standing erect, bar at shoulders.

Knowing how to breathe properly will add a lot to your lifting. What to remember in general is to inhale during the easier part of the movement, and to exhale while putting your muscles through the hard work. Any special instructions for breathing during a particular exercise will be mentioned during the description for that exercise.

Finally, be sure to go through each weightlifting movement as instructed. It's easy to cheat by bringing muscles into play that weren't intended for a particular exercise. Don't do it! You get the most benefit from your workouts when you lift the right way.

## Strengthening Your Legs

There are several lifts to help you own a pair of powerful legs. Almost all of them require the barbell to be held at the back of your shoulders, so an assistant or partner may be helpful for leg workouts. You don't need a partner if the bar is light enough for you to clean and press over your head, allowing you to get it onto your shoulders. Most gymnasiums have barbell racks, either as stands or attached to a wall, just so lifters can easily get a bar onto their shoulders.

### Squats

Squatting with a barbell is one of the best builders of leg strength. The squat, as pointed out in Chapter 4, is simply a deep knee bend. But with weights, squats are made more difficult by the added resistance of a barbell resting on your shoulders.

Get the bar in position so that it rests comfortably on a meaty part of your shoulders. Set your feet about shoulder-width apart, stand with a nearly erect stance, and look forward so your head is up. Fix your eyes on a spot on the ceiling. Take a deep breath and dip down, exhaling, until the tops of your thighs are parallel to the floor. Your feet should still be flat on the floor. Then, without bouncing, quickly rise out of the bottom position using the power in your legs. Rise with an erect back, still exhaling, and with your

**Keep your head up and back straight when squatting. Squat down until your thighs are parallel to the floor.**

eyes still fixed on a particular spot on the ceiling. An important part of squatting is keeping your back as straight as possible and your head up.

In the first part of the movement, *be sure not to go too low.* Any time you squat below the position of thighs level with the floor, an unnecessary strain is put on the knees. Squatting down to the parallel position is considered a full squat that works the quadriceps, hamstrings, and gluteus maximi as well as they need.

### Front Squats

Squatting with the bar held in front of your shoulders is a great exercise for building up the tops of your thighs. Front squats may also be the way for you to squat when there is no assistant to help get the bar on the back of your shoulders.

Clean the bar and hold it at your upper chest just below your neck. Squat with the bar, going only low enough so that the tops of your thighs are level with the floor. At that point, push up and out of the squat position with your legs. As with rear squats, begin with your lungs full and exhale during the entire movement. Be sure to keep your head up and your back straight.

Start a front squat with the bar at your upper chest. Squat down until your thighs are level with the floor.

## Step-Ups

Long-distance runners often do step-ups to help strengthen their legs for marathons. This exercise is done by stepping up onto a sturdy bench or stool 12 to 15 inches (30 to 40 cm) high. Use a barbell with about half the weight you can squat with. Place the bench before you and put the barbell on the back of your

With bar on shoulders, prepare to step up. Stand up on the bench for a second, balanced.

shoulders. Then, with one leg at a time, step up on the bench until your leg is straight and quickly come back down. Alternate legs while doing step-ups.

## Calf Raises

A block of wood about 1 to 2 inches (2 to 5 cm) thick is needed for this exercise. Start as you would for a squat by placing the barbell on your back. When you're set, put your feet on the blocks so that the heels hang off and are lower. Then, rise up and down on the balls of your feet. It won't take very many reps to make your calves feel like they're on fire. In fact, you may want to get in shape for this exercise by doing it several times without the added weight of the barbell.

## Leg Extensions

Even though it's special equipment, a leg extension machine is needed for leg extensions, but the exercise is important to point out. Leg extensions work your legs from a different angle than squats do and you may care enough to invest in the apparatus or find a gym that has one.

With weight added to the machine, simply sit on the edge of the bench, lock one foot (or both feet) behind the roller, and straighten your leg. Lower your foot and repeat to give your quadriceps a workout.

**With a leg extension machine, raise the weights with your thigh muscles.**

# Building Up the Back

Because the back is the center of all body movement, it really pays to build up the muscles there. These five weightlifting exercises include all you need to strengthen every part of your back.

### Deadlifts

The deadlift works both the lower and upper parts of the back. It simply requires that you lift a barbell from the floor to your hips. Start with your feet about shoulder-width or a little wider and grasp the bar with one hand around the bar palm up, and the other hand around palm down. Lower your buttocks to get set, take a deep breath, and begin the pull. At first, use driving leg force to raise the bar. About halfway up, your back will take over much of the pull. Exhale throughout the entire lift. Stand erect to complete the deadlift, lower the bar, and repeat. Even by using your legs for much of the lift, your back still gets a good workout.

### Stiff-Legged Deadlifts

There's little use of the legs in this exercise, so it really concentrates on the back muscles—this makes the stiff-legged deadlift the most thorough exercise for the lower back. First pick up a barbell in deadlift style using your legs and the proper grip. Once you're standing erect, lower the weight by bending at the waist only, and touch the barbell to the floor. Then straighten up again, but without using your legs—keep them straight. Remember that this is an all-back movement. Start stiff-legged deadlifts with a light weight to determine the condition of your back muscles.

### Bent-Over Rowing

This exercise gives a workout to all parts of your back. Bend over at the waist and pick up a barbell from the floor. Let it hang from your extended arms while you remain bent over. Use

Use reversed grips for the deadlift. With both legs and back muscles, bring the bar up to your hips.

your arms to pull the bar up as close to your chest as possible, (see photos), then lower it. Even though your arms are doing much of the work, the middle back still bears quite a load in this exercise.

## Shoulder Shrugs

Doing a shrugging movement while holding a barbell exercises the traps at the base of your neck. Hold the barbell at your hips with an overhand grip so that the weight of the bar pulls your shoulder down (see below). Now, with only the upward movement of your shoulders, raise the bar as far as possible, which will only be a few inches, hold for a few seconds, and then lower the barbell to the starting position. You can also do shoulder shrugs with heavy dumbbells.

## Cleans

As described on page 88, cleaning a barbell is the fundamental weightlifting movement needed to get the barbell up to your shoulders. Cleaning is also an excellent back exercise by itself.

**For the shoulder shrug, first let the bar hang, then shrug your shoulders so you feel it in your neck.**

Although the legs are largely used, much of the strength needed for cleans comes from the lower back muscles.

## Developing the Chest

A well-developed chest means not only strength, but increased lung capacity as well. Good breathing rhythm is important here. In any chest exercise, inhale during the part that expands your pectoral muscles.

**For the bench press, hold the bar above your chest, lower it, and press it up again.**

### Bench Presses

The best chest developer of all is the bench press. This movement requires either having a bench with racks for the barbell or an assistant to hand you the bar. In either case, *have a spotter stand behind you while you bench press.*

To perform this exercise, lie on your back on a bench. Reach up to remove the bar from the racks or have your partner hand it to you. Hold it with extended arms over your head, using a grip anywhere from shoulder-width to about 12 inches (30 cm) wider. Be certain to wrap your thumbs around the bar. Lower

**A press on an inclined bench helps work your upper chest.**

the bar, breathing in to expand your chest. Touch the bar lightly to your chest and press it back up fully. Keep your feet flat on the floor and your buttocks on the bench throughout the entire movement or muscles other than those of your chest will come into play and your pectorals won't get as good a workout. Besides the pectorals, the bench press helps in the development of the shoulders and upper arms.

### Inclined Bench Presses

If you can construct or purchase an inclined board or a bench, you can do bench presses that directly work your upper chest. Usually two spotters are needed for inclined bench presses to hand you the bar. As with regular "benches," lower the bar from an extended-arm position, lightly touch your chest, and press upward. Inhale on the descent and exhale while pressing. The wider your grip, the more the pressing effort is placed on your chest muscles rather than on your upper arms (triceps).

## Dumbbell Bench Presses

Here, an ordinary bench will do. Lie on the bench and hold a dumbbell in each hand over your chest with straight arms. Lower the dumbbells in a vertical path as far as your chest muscles permit, breathing in throughout the movement. Then press the bells straight up in good form, exhaling until completion. You may choose to use this chest-developer regularly instead of the barbell bench press.

You can use dumbbells instead of a bar for bench presses.

**Start with bells above your chest and lower them, using your pectoral muscles.**

## Laterals

This exercise, sometimes called "flyes," will really stretch out and build up your pecs. Lie on a bench and hold a dumbbell in each hand with your arms straight over your chest. Now spread your arms apart as though they were wings, inhaling and lowering the weights until your arms are parallel with the floor, and even lower if your chest muscles comfortably allow it. Then, with the strength of your pectorals, bring the dumbbells together again overhead, exhaling while doing so. Depending on the weight you use, you can do these laterals with either straight arms or your elbows bent. In addition, you can do straight-arm and bent-arm laterals on an incline board or bench.

## Pullovers

This is one of the tougher chest exercises, but well worth the effort. It not only helps chest development, but also works the upper back and shoulders. Lie on the bench or on the floor. If you use a bench, put your feet flat on the floor or locked around the bench legs. If you lie on the floor, lie straight with your legs extended. Hold a light barbell with straight arms over your chest with a shoulder-width grip. Keep your arms straight and lower the barbell over and in back of your head until your arms are level with the floor. Inhale throughout this movement.

**Try pullovers at the end of a bench.**

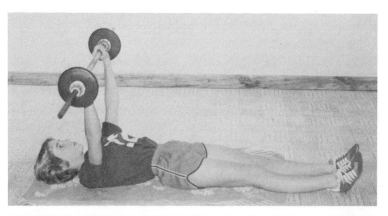

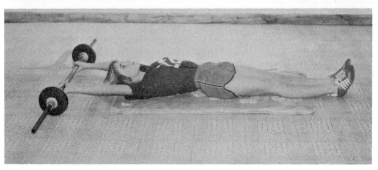

For pullovers, hold the bar above you and gradually lower
it backwards until it touches the floor behind you.

Return the weight by pulling it up and over your head to its starting position above your chest. Exhale while pulling up. An alternate way to do pullovers is with bent arms on a bench or you can use dumbbells instead of a barbell.

## Shaping Up the Shoulders

Any sort of pulling or pushing action calls on strength from the shoulders. Barbells and dumbbells offer more than half a dozen good ways to strengthen these body parts.

**A military press begins at the shoulders.**
**Press the bar directly overhead.**

### Military Presses

A popular exercise, the military press is a prime means of developing shoulder power. Clean the barbell to your shoulders, keeping in mind the proper way to clean, as discussed on page 88. Pause, then push the bar up until your arms are fully extended overhead. Lower the bar to shoulder level and repeat. You can do military presses standing or sitting on a bench.

**Put the bar on the backs of your shoulders and press up behind
your head.**

### Presses Behind the Neck

This is a variation of the military press, but it concentrates
more on the back of the shoulders than the regular "militaries" do.
Place a barbell behind your neck on the back of your shoulders,
or have an assistant put it there for you, and hold it with palms
facing forward. Press the bar up until your arms are fully extended
overhead. Lower the bar to your shoulders and repeat. Like the
military presses, you can do this press standing or seated.

**Press dumbbells instead of a barbell.**

## Dumbbell Presses

Pressing dumbbells over your head rather than a barbell puts a little more demand on the sides of the shoulders. Dumbbell presses can be done standing, seated by pressing one arm at a time, or by pressing left and right arms simultaneously or alternately.

**In upright rowing, let the bar hang from extended arms.
Use your shoulder power to raise it directly up.**

## Upright Rowing

This exercise gives a thorough workout to the entire shoulder region. Hold the barbell at your hips with arms extended, and with either a wide or narrow grip. Pull the barbell directly up parallel to your body as far as possible and then lower it. Maintain a smooth pull throughout the movement and keep the bar close to your body. This exercise resembles rowing a boat, therefore the name "upright rowing." Besides helping the shoulders, this rowing action greatly assists the traps at the base of your neck and tops of your shoulders.

## Front Lateral Raises

This exercise calls for and develops strength in the front deltoids. Hold a barbell at your hips with arms extended downward. Then, with only the strength of your shoulders, raise the weight forward until your arms are at least parallel to the floor. You can also do front raises with dumbbells, raising both arms

**Begin the front lateral raise with a bar before you and raise it forward using your deltoid muscles. You can use dumbbells for lateral raises also.**

together or alternately. For stricter control, do front lateral raises with dumbbells while seated on the edge of a bench.

### Side Lateral Raises

To give a workout to the side deltoids, raise the dumbbells out from the sides of your body with arms straight. Lift the weights high enough so that your arms are level with the floor, then lower the weight to your hips and repeat. Side lateral raises can be done one arm at a time, two arms simultaneously, or with dumbbells parallel or perpendicular to the floor.

**For side laterals, raise dumbbells outwards.**

### Bent-Over Lateral Raises

The best exercise for the rear shoulder muscles is lateral raises with dumbbells while leaning over. Take a dumbbell in each hand and bend over at the waist, letting the weights hang from your arms. Use the muscles at the back of your shoulders to raise the dumbbells up so that your arms are parallel to the floor. Lower the weights and repeat.

In the bent-over lateral raise, first let the dumbbells hang, then spread them outward, using your shoulder strength.

## Activating the Arms

The two muscle groups to strengthen in the arms are the biceps and the triceps. When pulling, pushing, or pressing, the triceps play the bigger role, so direct at least as much attention there as toward the biceps.

### Curls

Barbell curls are without a doubt the most popular of arm exercises. Simply hold a barbell at your hips with a shoulder-width palms-up grip. Curl the bar to touch your shoulders and lower it back down. To do a biceps curl properly, keep your back straight and concentrate on using only your upper arms to curl the bar. When lowering the bar, remain firm and resist the pull of the bar on your arms.

Curls are the most popular arm exercise. Start with palms-up grip, and curl the bar up to your upper chest (above). Also try curls with a reverse grip (left).

### Reverse Curls

The difference between these curls and regular curls are the grip and the muscles used. Here, the grip is palms down. Curling the bar up to your shoulders in this fashion will put a lot of demand on the backs of your forearms as well as the biceps.

### Dumbbell Curls

To get a somewhat different movement for the curling exercise, use dumbbells instead of a barbell. With dumbbells you can curl standing, seated, or on an incline. Exercise each arm, alternately or both arms simultaneously.

## Narrow-Grip Bench Presses

Although the bench press is mainly a chest exercise, you can use a narrow grip while "benching" to place most of the burden on your triceps. Except for the close spacing of the hands, this movement is performed just like a normal bench press (page 97). Pick the bar off a rack at the head of the bench or have it handed to you, lower it to touch your chest, and press it fully upward. It's a good idea to use a spotter for this one.

**(Left) Curling a heavy dumbbell is excellent for biceps. (Right) For triceps, do bench presses with a narrow grip.**

## Triceps Extensions

This exercise isolates the triceps well for a solid workout— provided you can keep your elbows stationary. Sit on the edge of a bench and hold a dumbbell behind your neck. Then, without moving your elbow, raise the weight above the back of your head and lower it. If the dumbbell has bolts holding a plate collar on, be sure they're tight before doing triceps extensions. You can also do this movement with a barbell by holding it with a narrow grip either seated or standing.

**To extend your triceps, hold a dumbbell behind your head, then raise it up, using your triceps only.**

**Try triceps extensions with a barbell.**

# Key Points for Successful Lifting

■ Have respect for the weights. Never attempt to lift a weight that you know is too heavy to be within your ability to handle.

■ In general, inhale while doing the easier part of an exercise and exhale during the strenuous movement. For example, when pressing, exhale as you press the bar overhead and inhale as you lower it to your shoulders.

■ Warm up before lifting heavy weights. This will be discussed in the next section.

■ Dress warmly in cool weather, and stay out of air currents in warm weather.

■ *Do not* bench press alone. Use a spotter or have an assistant nearby.

■ When cleaning a weight, keep your back flat and drive with your legs. Pull on the bar so that it rises vertically.

■ When squatting, keep your head up and your back as straight as possible. Also, *do not* go below parallel with your thighs or bounce on your knees.

■ Keep your head up and your back as straight as possible when deadlifting. Drive with your legs.

■ In any exercise, *do not* bring muscles into play that were not intended to be. For example, when curling a barbell, don't assist the curl by leaning backwards.

## The Exercises

Select one exercise for each body part per workout.

| Body parts and exercises | Early teens (13–15 years) sets/reps | Late teens (16–19 years) sets/reps | Post-teens sets/reps |
|---|---|---|---|
| **LEGS** | | | |
| Squats | 3/8–10 | 3–4/5–10 | 3–5/5–10 |
| Front Squats | 3/8–10 | 3–4/5–10 | 3–5/5–10 |
| Step-ups | 2/8–10 | 2–4/5–10 | 3–5/5–10 |
| Calf raises | 2/10–15 | 2–4/10–20 | 3–5/10–20 |
| Leg extensions | 2/10 | 2–4/10 | 3–5/10 |
| **BACK** | | | |
| Deadlifts | 3/5–7 | 3–4/5–7 | 3–5/5–10 |
| Stiff-legged deadlifts | 2/5–7 | 2–4/5–7 | 3–5/5–10 |
| Bent-over rowing | 2/8–10 | 2–4/8–10 | 3–5/8–10 |
| Shoulder shrugs | 2/8–10 | 2–4/10–20 | 3–5/10–20 |
| Cleans | 2/5–7 | 2–4/5–7 | 3–5/5–10 |

## CHEST

| Exercise | | | |
|---|---|---|---|
| Bench presses | 3/5-8 | 3-4/5-8 | 5/5-10 |
| Inclined bench presses | 2/5-7 | 3/5-7 | 3-5/5-10 |
| Dumbbell bench presses | 3/7-10 | 3-4/8-10 | 5/8-10 |
| Laterals | 2/7-10 | 3/8-10 | 3-5/8-10 |
| Pullovers | 2/5-8 | 3/5-8 | 3-5/5-10 |

## SHOULDERS

| Exercise | | | |
|---|---|---|---|
| Military presses | 3/5-7 | 3-4/5-7 | 3-5/5-8 |
| Behind-the-neck presses | 2/5-7 | 2-4/5-7 | 3-5/5-8 |
| Dumbbell presses | 3/5-7 | 3-4/5-7 | 3-5/5-10 |
| Upright rowing | 2/8-10 | 2-4/8-10 | 3-5/8-10 |
| Front laterals | 2/5-8 | 3/6-8 | 3/7-10 |
| Side laterals | 2/5-8 | 3/6-8 | 3/7-10 |
| Bent-over laterals | 2/5-8 | 3/6-8 | 3/7-10 |

## ARMS

| Exercise | | | |
|---|---|---|---|
| Curls | 3/5-8 | 3-4/5-10 | 3-5/5-10 |
| Reverse curls | 2/5-7 | 2-4/6-8 | 3-5/6-8 |
| Dumbbell curls | 3/6-8 | 3-4/8-10 | 3-5/8-10 |
| Narrow-grip bench presses | 2/5-7 | 2-4/6-8 | 3-5/6-8 |
| Triceps extensions | 2/6-8 | 2-4/8-10 | 3-5/8-10 |

## Sample Regimens

| Monday | Wednesday | Friday |
|--------|-----------|--------|
| Squats | Deadlifts | Squats |
| Bench presses | Laterals | Bench presses |
| Bent-over rowing | Calf raises | Bent-over rowing |
| Military presses | Behind-the-neck presses | Military presses |
| Curls | Curls | Curls |
| | | |
| Front squats | Stiff-legged deadlifts | Front squats |
| Bench presses | Pullovers | Bench presses |
| Bent-over rowing | Calf raises | Bent-over rowing |
| Shoulder shrugs | Shoulder shrugs | Shoulder shrugs |
| Reverse curls | Curls | Reverse curls |
| | | |
| Squats | Deadlifts | Squats |
| Bench presses | Pullovers | Bench presses |
| Cleans | Step-ups | Cleans |
| Laterals | Laterals | Laterals |
| Dumbbell curls | Curls | Dumbbell curls |

Front squats
Stiff-legged deadlifts
Dumbbell bench presses
Upright rowing
Narrow-grip bench presses

Squats
Bent-over rowing
Laterals
Behind-the-neck presses
Curls

Cleans
Calf raises
Bench presses
Upright rowing
Curls

Cleans
Step-ups
Laterals
Upright rowing
Triceps extensions

Front squats
Stifflegged deadlifts
Dumbbell bench presses
Upright rowing
Narrow-grip bench presses

Squats
Bent-over rowing
Laterals
Behind-the-neck presses
Curls

Add sit-ups (while holding a weight plate behind your head) to any of these regimens.

# Your Weightlifting Regimen for Growing Strong

Probably the biggest question on your mind about weightlifting is "How much weight should I use for each exercise?" Actually, there's no exact answer to this question. The weight that you select and the weights that feel light, medium and heavy to you depend on your present size and strength. When it comes to choosing the right weight for each exercise, it's as personal as selecting the sizes and styles of your clothing. That is, no one can tell you how much weight to begin with—what's heavy to you may feel like a sack of feathers to another person.

Before doing any exercise for the first time, experiment to determine just how many pounds will be comfortable for you to use. Start light and gradually work up in weight. A weight with which you can do 5 to 7 reps, depending on the exercise, is a good one to start with.

The best workout schedule for weightlifting is every other day, 3 days a week. Monday-Wednesday-Friday routines are the most common among lifters in strength training. You can, of course, increase your strength lifting only 2 days a week, especially if you combine lifting with another activity, such as aerobics. But three days a week is best—especially for making strength progress when lifting only. Remember, too, that part of growing up strong is having enough rest days in your schedule. Always allow two days in a row, such as the weekends, for your body to thoroughly recover.

The time of day you work out is not very important, but try to be consistent in your time from session to session. Always remember to let a meal digest for about two hours before lifting weights.

The amount of time you devote to each workout, including warm-ups and shower, should be no longer than one hour. This is plenty of time to accomplish all that you need for remaining on track with your growing-strong regimen. Early teenagers, however, will not even need an hour because their workout loads are relatively light.

To finish within one hour, set a pace to your workouts. This depends a lot on the time you allow for resting between sets. It should be long enough to recover from the previous set so that you can perform the next one in good form, but don't overdo the resting time. Long breaks let your body cool down, which in turn makes you vulnerable to strains. In general, breaks between sets should be less than 2 minutes but at least 15 seconds long.

Not all exercises should be performed 3 days a week. Some that use major muscle groups, like deadlifts and squats, need only be done once or twice a week. Others, such as arm and shoulder exercises, can be performed at each workout. The mid-week workout for the 3-day-a-week schedule should be a little lighter than on the first and third sessions of the week. Either use slightly less weight, or do fewer reps. The reason for variations in the weekly regimen is that you can't expect your muscles to perform at their best for 3 workouts each week—this could lead to overtraining. That is, you could reach a point where strength progress stops. You need to offer resistance to your muscles 3 days a week, but you can't test their limits at every session.

The system recommended for building up strength is progressive. You'll gradually train your muscles to handle more and heavier loads by gradually increasing the weight you use. From the chart provided for this progressive system, select at least one exercise per workout for each body area—legs, back, chest, shoulders and arms. If you choose to do more than one exercise per body part during a workout, don't duplicate certain movements. That is, don't perform more than one type of squat, deadlift, bench press, press, or curl during the same workout. You can do more than one type of lateral raise, however, because each works different muscles.

Sample routines are given to get you started. Stay with one for a while, but over a period of time, try all of the exercises discussed in this chapter in your routine. See which are more enjoyable and increase your strength the most. For variety, you may want to make changes in your regimen once every month or two.

For sensible and progressive strength training, do the number of sets per exercise for your age group and try to achieve the maximum number of suggested reps. Remember, however, to use a lighter weight or to do a lower number of reps once a week for any exercise you do 3 days a week. When you can perform the required sets at the maximum reps for a week's workout, increase the weight. For large muscle groups like the legs and back, a 10-pound (5-kg) increase may be in order, but for the smaller muscle groups, adding 5 pounds (2.5 kg) should be enough.

The one major body part not discussed in this chapter is the stomach region, the abdominal muscles. The reason, of course, is that you can't use a weight directly for strengthening this area. You can, however, use a weight plate when you do sit-ups (as described on page 71). Hold a 5- or 10-pound plate (2.5-kg or 5-kg plate) behind your neck and do about 10 sit-ups. The added resistance will increase the strength of your abdominals.

Begin each workout with proper warming up and stretching—this is important for both beginning and experienced lifters. Many competitive weightlifters, for example, spend 10 to 15 minutes going through a warm-up and stretching routine before practice or competition. For your training, about 5 minutes of pre-workout activity should be enough. Use the information in Chapter 2 for examples and instructions for loosening up. Good exercises to use before weightlifting are:

Side bends—10 reps.

Twisting—10 reps.

Shoulder rotations—10 reps.

Toe touches and back bends—10 reps.

Lunges—5 reps.

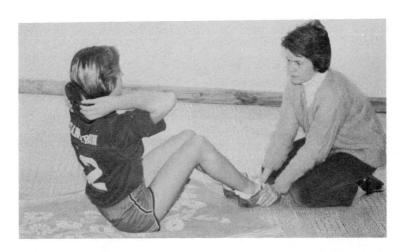

**When doing sit-ups, hold a weight plate behind your head.**

Knee bends (squats)—10–15 reps.

Jogging in place—1 minute.

You don't have to do all of these movements before a particular workout. Experiment with them to decide which leave you best prepared for the weightlifting routine you choose. A satisfying warm-up should cause you to perspire a bit and leave you physically loose, energetic and mentally ready to get into your weightlifting routine.

As a final word of caution, remember not to become too ambitious. Three days a week of weightlifting, one hour each session, is plenty. Doing any more may only defeat your purpose by keeping your body in a state of fatigue. Also, be sure to get 7 to 9 hours of sleep each night. Adequate rest is essential for building strength.

# Questions and Answers

*I'm 15 years old and have been lifting weights for about a year. My strength has increased a great deal, but I seem to have reached a point in a few exercises where I no longer make progress. What can I do to get over these slumps and begin making more progress?*

What you're referring to are "sticking points," where there seems to be some invisible barrier holding back your progress. A good way around sticking points is to cut back on the number of reps and add weight. Then once you can work the heavier weight at lowered reps, you should be able to do a higher number of reps at the weight you were sticking at earlier.

*You mentioned overtraining. Could you say a little more about that?*

It's possible to work too hard. The result is a lack of progress, or maybe even a decrease in strength. A strength athlete tries to find the delicate balance between too much training and too little. That is, after becoming advanced, each person must find how much training is just right. Just remember that a whole lot of something is not always better.

*It seems that a person may reach a point where he uses weights so heavy that expecting to perform 8 or 10 reps may be too much. Is that true?*

Yes. An experienced lifter who works out with heavy weights may only do 3 or 5 reps each set. In fact, true strength is built by occasionally performing heavy "singles," or sets of one rep. But leave that to the experts who have many years of lifting behind them.

*My older brother has a buddy who works out 6 days a week. Why didn't you recommend that?*

That fellow is undoubtedly into bodybuilding, a sport where weights are used to sculpture muscular physiques. Many bodybuilders do work out nearly every day, but they're seeking goals different from those outlined here. Moreover, serious bodybuilders usually have 5 or 10 years of lifting behind them and they treat their sport almost like a full-time job. The regimens here provide solid, lasting strength without interfering with your other activities.

*You didn't mention the lifts known as the clean and jerk and the snatch. What are those?*

These are special lifts used in the type of competitive weightlifting known as Olympic lifting. They're explained in detail in *Competitive Weightlifting* (Sterling Publishing Co. Inc.). Each involves a special technique for lifting a barbell over your head and holding it there for about 2 seconds.

*Is there a difference in the results between using a heavy weight at low reps and using a light weight for many reps?*

Yes. Usually a lot of reps increases one's endurance more than strength. Heavy but lesser reps helps to increase strength more than endurance. The regimens here are for a balance between endurance and strength.

# Chapter 6

# EATING RIGHT FOR A SOLID FOUNDATION

You may, some day, own a very expensive automobile. You'll probably expect it to perform better than most all other cars on the roads. But whether or not your car works well depends a lot on how you treat it. If you feed it low-quality fuel, the car will run sluggishly and probably have a short life span. Or, without any fuel, the car has no chance of performing at all.

Your body works much the same way. It needs "fuel" to perform—for energy and for growth. And that fuel to run on should be high in quality and come in the form of nutritious food. The food that you eat is as important a part of growing up strong as the exercises that you do.

Foods are a major part of our everyday lives. But what makes one food more nutritious than another? Why does roast beef, for example, make a more nourishing meal than a pizza? Or why is milk considered an important part of every meal whereas cola is not? The answers lie in the amounts of *nutrients* in each food. Nutrients are the substances in foods which are necessary for the functioning of any living body. They are the materials that provide the fuel for energy, the building blocks for body growth and strength, and they help to control natural body processes.

There are 5 major groups of nutrients—carbohydrates, fats,

proteins, minerals, vitamins—and a sixth if water is included. Each nutrient group has a special role in growing up strong.

## Get Your Energy from Carbohydrates and Fats

Nearly all of the energy you "burn" comes from two nutrients, carbohydrates and fats. The amount of energy these nutrients provide is measured in *kilocalories,* a unit physicists use for measuring heat. One kilocalorie equals the amount of heat necessary to raise the temperature of 1 kilogram of water by 1 degree Centigrade. In this way, kilocalories measure the energy content of foods. Each day, young people and adults each burn over 2000 kilocalories. Your activities in aerobics, exercises or weightlifting mean that carbohydrates and fats should be important parts of your daily diet.

Our largest source of carbohydrates is in the plant foods we eat, such as corn, potatoes, rice, wheat, and fruits. In these products, carbohydrates are present as sugars, starches, and cellulose. For example, it is the sugars, *fructose* and *glucose,* that give fruits their appealing tastes and supply us with carbohydrates. One important animal source of carbohydrates is milk and milk products. There, the energy is found as the sugars *lactose* and *galactose.*

The most abundant carbohydrate in the diets of the world population is starch. Popular sources are the cereal grains—wheat, corn, and rice. The carbohydrate cellulose is also a big part of most diets, but your body can't digest it for energy. Rather, cellulose serves as bulk that aids in keeping digestive systems in good working order.

Fats are the most concentrated form of food energy, containing more than twice as much energy than an equal weight of carbohydrate. In addition to providing fuel for immediate energy, fats serve as the main supply of stored, or reserve, energy. The storage areas are located under the skin as *adipose tissue.* Clearly, too much fat accumulating beneath the skin leads to overweight problems.

There are two main types of fats that we eat: vegetable fat and animal fat. In either case, fat is a greasy or oily substance that does not dissolve in water. Good examples of vegetable fat are margarine and cooking oil. Other foods that contain nourishing amounts of vegetable fats are peanuts, peanut butter, seeds, and nuts. Easily recognized, animal fat is the white portion of bacon, although animal fat is also found in beef, poultry, fish, eggs, and milk products.

## There's Power in Protein

Protein is the real key to success in strength. This nutrient serves to grow new muscle and tissue and to replace worn-down body parts. Protein is a true body builder. Any aerobics, exercise, or weightlifting regimen calls for hearty amounts of protein in the diet.

Besides composing much of your muscle tissue, protein is also a large part of your connective tissue, such as the *ligaments* which hold your bones together at the joints and the *tendons* which attach your muscles to your bones. And in your blood, protein is present as hemoglobin, the substance that carries oxygen from lungs to muscles. Proteins are also found in the blood as antibodies, the defenders against disease.

Scientists tell us that proteins are made up of even smaller parts —chemical building blocks called *amino acids*. Twenty-two amino acids are commonly found in proteins, all of which are absolutely necessary for body growth and maintenance. Your body, though, is able to chemically convert some amino acids into others so that if one amino acid is temporarily in short supply, it can be made from another amino acid present in larger amounts. There are, however, eight amino acids that your body can't produce this way, and you must have enough of all of them in your diet so that you never run short. Nutritionists refer to those eight as the *essential* amino acids.

Proteins that contain all eight essential amino acids are called *complete* proteins. If the protein doesn't have all eight, it's considered incomplete. Only complete protein is capable of maintaining life, supporting growth, and building strength.

There are a variety of foods that contain complete protein. Almost any animal product is a good source—meats, poultry, fish, eggs, milk, and the dairy products (cheese, cottage cheese, yogurt). On the other hand, most grains, nuts and vegetables have lower-quality, or incomplete proteins. There is one important exception, however, and that is the soybean. This vegetable has abundant protein that is as high in quality as meat protein.

Grain, nut, and vegetable proteins are still useful to your well-being. By combining incomplete proteins with complete ones, such as eating cereal with milk, you can fully utilize all the protein content in each food.

## Staying Healthy with Minerals and Vitamins

All the exercise in the world would not help you if you didn't receive minerals from your diet. Many minerals, such as calcium and phosphorus, make up the hard parts of your body—bones and teeth. Certainly without those solid bones, there wouldn't be much foundation on which to build strength. Other minerals, like iron, magnesium, sodium, potassium, and chlorine, play important roles in the compositions of muscles, blood, and glands. Still others are necessary in certain body functions, such as the operation of muscle cells.

A good share of the minerals needed for growth and strength are found in the same foods that provide body-building proteins. That is, dairy products, meats and grains are major sources, but in addition, green leafy vegetables supply necessary minerals.

The same holds true for the sources of vitamins, although fruits must be added to the list here. Vitamins are compounds in foods that are required for growth, for the utilization of other nutrients, and for the prevention of diseases. With any of the vitamins (A, B-complex, C, D, E, or K) missing from your diet, illnesses are sure to develop.

# Avoid Those Junk Foods

The amount of nutrients in foods varies greatly from one product to another. Some, like milk and soybeans, are rich in all nutrients—carbohydrates, fats, proteins, minerals, and vitamins. They are almost complete foods within themselves. Others, like green vegetables, may be strong in only two or three nutrients, such as carbohydrates, vitamins, and minerals. But some foods have really nothing to contribute to your health.

Sugar is the best example. It's true that sugar is a carbohydrate and provides calories for energy, but that is all. Because of this, sugar has earned a reputation of being "empty calories" or "foodless food." And on top of that, recent scientific studies have related eating too much sugar with the occurrence of heart diseases in adults.

Other foods have poor reputations, too. Any product made from white flour (as opposed to whole wheat flour), like white breads and most pastries, is "foodless food." They have little more to offer than carbohydrates. Many breakfast cereals also fall under this category, being made largely from sugar and from grains that food processors have robbed of most of their original nutrients.

The danger of junk foods in a regimen of growing up strong is that they can easily replace nourishing foods in one's diet. Junk food will give you calories for energy, but nothing else for your health and strength. A good example of this may occur at breakfast. In some homes, sugar-rich cereals take the place of a nourishing grain product. If you're going to begin your day with cereal carbohydrates, you should receive significant amounts of other nutrients, such as protein and minerals, at the same time.

Your regimen of growing up strong doesn't have to entirely exclude all junk foods. To be realistic, few people can be so rigid. After all, the sugar in such foods as soda and cake makes them appealing to our tastes. Most important is that you recognize the nutritious foods and give those first place in your diet—and avoid those junk foods as much as possible.

## Key Points for Good Nutrition

- For energy from carbohydrates, eat grains, fruits, vegetables and dairy products.

- For energy from fats, eat nuts, seeds, and dairy products.

- For muscle-building protein, eat meat, poultry, fish, dairy products, and soybeans.

- For strengthening bones and teeth, drink and eat dairy products for the minerals calcium and phosphorous.

- For vitamins, include ample meats, grains, dairy products, fruits, and vegetables.

- Stay away from sugar-rich foods (candy bars, pastries, sugar-rich sodas, certain commercial pastries and cereals). These products only spoil your appetite and keep you from eating nutritious foods.

## Your Diet for Growing Strong

Nutritionists say that an adequate diet is one that contains all the necessary nutrients in proper amounts. In terms of the dinner table, this means you need to eat servings from 4 food groups at each meal: milk, meat, vegetable-fruit, and cereal. These categories offer a wide choice of different foods to serve in a variety of meals with abundant nutrients.

In addition to making the 4-group plan part of your daily diet, you also need good eating habits. You should eat 3 solid meals a day and perhaps a few nutritious snacks. It's also wise to distribute the nutrients over the day, not eating nearly all at only one or two meals. This will keep you supplied with a steady flow of nourishment. And it's especially important that you don't miss any meals.

Start each day with a wholesome breakfast. Eat fruit or drink a glass of fruit or vegetable juice. Oranges, grapefruits, peaches, pears and cantaloupes are good choices for fruits. For juice, consider grapefruit, orange, pineapple or tomato. Eat a bowl of a whole-grain cereal or toast or muffins made from whole-grain flour. Instead of grain food, you could eat one or two eggs or meat like bacon or ham. Drink at least one cup of milk, either with cereal or served alone. Your choice in milk could be whole milk, skim milk, powdered milk, or buttermilk; all are equally nourishing.

Whether you eat lunch at home, work, or school, a good mid-day meal should consist of one or two sandwiches made from whole-grain bread and protein-rich filling such as meat, cheese or peanut butter. Good substitutes for a sandwich are yogurt or cottage cheese. Vegetables like raw carrots or celery or a bowl of green beans or peas should also be a part of lunch, or eat a fruit, such as an apple, orange or pear. Dessert can consist of a cookie or two, pudding, nuts or a serving of ice cream. Drink one to two glasses of milk.

The evening meal should be a good balance of meat, vegetable, and dairy products. A main course of beef, pork, chicken or fish, with a side dish of green beans, peas, broccoli, or spinach. A nourishing dessert could be pudding, pie, cake, or cottage cheese mixed with fruit. Include one or two cups of milk also.

Between-meal snacks can be an important part of a good diet, provided that they're wholesome and don't cause an overweight problem. Nuts, raw vegetables, fruits and yogurt are among the most healthful. Being active in a growing-up-strong regimen will call for an ample supply of calories from carbohydrates and fats, so don't hesitate to enjoy nutritious snacks with hearty amounts of these nutrients.

Above all else, the emphasis in your diet should be on protein. Where strength is involved, this is the sovereign nutrient. As a rule of thumb, remember that 1 gram (0.035 ounce) of complete protein should be eaten for every kilogram (2.2 pounds) of your bodyweight. That is, if you weigh 35 kilograms (77 pounds), eat about 35 grams (1¼ ounces) of protein daily.

## Carbohydrate content in 100 grams of certain foods
Source: Composition of Foods, USDA Handbook 8 (1963)

| Food | Carbohydrate, in grams |
| --- | --- |
| Sugar | 99.5 |
| Honey | 82.3 |
| Graham crackers | 73.3 |
| Jams | 70.0 |
| Bread (white) | 50.4 |
| Rice (white, cooked) | 24.0 |
| Apple | 14.5 |
| Soda pop (cola; 3½ ounces) | 10.0 |
| Milk (whole; 3½ ounces) | 4.9 |
| Cheese (cheddar) | 2.1 |
| Egg | 0.9 |
| Hamburger (cooked) | 0.0 |

## Fat content in 100 grams of certain foods
Source: Composition of Foods, USDA Handbook 8 (1963)

| Food | Fat, in grams |
| --- | --- |
| Oil (salad and cooking) | 100.0 |
| Butter | 81.0 |
| Walnuts | 59.3 |
| Potato chips | 39.3 |
| Bacon (fried) | 33.3 |
| Hamburger (cooked) | 20.7 |
| Egg | 11.5 |
| Ice cream | 10.6 |
| Graham crackers | 9.4 |
| Milk (whole; 3½ ounces) | 3.5 |
| Bread (white) | 3.2 |
| Sugar | 0.0 |

**Protein content in 100 grams of certain foods**
(Source: Composition of Foods, USDA Handbook 8 (1963)

| Food | Protein, in grams |
|------|-------------------|
| Soybeans (raw) | 34.1 |
| Chicken (cooked, no skin) | 31.6 |
| Peanut butter | 27.8 |
| Beef (chuck, cooked) | 26.0 |
| Tuna | 24.0 |
| Walnuts | 20.5 |
| Egg | 12.9 |
| Bread (white) | 8.7 |
| Ice cream | 4.0 |
| Milk (whole; $3\frac{1}{2}$ ounces) | 3.5 |
| Rice (white, cooked) | 2.0 |
| Sugar | 0.0 |

# Questions and Answers

*I've heard about food supplements—those protein powders taken to assure enough protein for building strength. Are they worth the money?*

Absolutely not. You can utilize only so much protein each day. If you eat grains, dairy products and meat each day in amounts of about 1 gram for every 1 kilogram (2 lb) of your bodyweight, there's no need for expensive protein powders or supplements of any kind to your diet.

*Just what are the most economical sources of protein?*

To get the most high-quality protein for your money, eat cottage cheese, soybeans, eggs, and drink powdered skim milk. Economical meat proteins are poultry and liver. Yogurt is an expensive source of protein unless you make it at home.

*What about vitamin tablets? Are they necessary?*

No supplements are needed if you eat a nourishing, well-balanced diet each day. But for a few pennies a day, it may be a good idea to take a multi-vitamin tablet if you have any doubt about receiving all the important vitamins each day.

*Some foods are labelled as fortified or enriched. What's been done to the original food and is this good or bad for nutrition?*

"Fortified" is most commonly found printed on milk cartons and on cereal boxes. It means that minerals or vitamins that were never in the product to begin with have been added by food processors. In the case of milk, vitamin D is added. "Enriched" means that more of a nutrient originally present in a product has been added. Often times though, as in the case of white bread, a nutrient like vitamin B (niacin) is removed first for processing purposes, and then added later—the bread becomes enriched in niacin. In most cases, fortification and enrichment are to the betterment of products.

*I'm not much of a meat eater. Does this mean I'll have difficulty getting enough protein?*

No. Eat a lot of dairy products, like cheese, cottage cheese and milk. Don't overlook soybeans either—a mainstay of protein in some Eastern countries.

*You mentioned that water is a sixth major nutrient. How is that?*

Water is essential for digestion and for elimination and must be present in all body tissues. Each person needs several glasses a day. Much of this is obtained through fruits and vegetables which are to a large extent composed of water. When working out or on hot days, you may easily perspire more than a quart (1 litre) of water. So don't hesitate to drink a lot.

# Chapter 7

# TAKING CARE OF
# THOSE SORE SPOTS

Almost any course you choose for growing up strong will from time to time bring a few aches and pains along with it. Even by taking proper care to stretch and loosen up before working out, you may still suffer a mild injury or minor ailment. It may come from an accident or fall that twists an ankle or pulls a muscle, or you may just work out too hard. Fortunately, the only ailment most people suffer is sore muscles, which is not a serious problem. This usually happens when beginning a regimen or when returning to one after a long time off. But whatever the injuries or problems affecting your strength regimen, it's good to know what to do about them so you can quickly and safely return to your training.

Keep in mind that this is not a medical book. We intend only to help you with some home remedies for minor injuries. If you seriously injure yourself, see your doctor. And, in the event of a severe injury, *do not* continue with your normal workouts until fully recovered.

Some people become too enthusiastic about physical fitness and refuse to modify their exercise schedules when injured or ill. Long-distance runners often overexert themselves while hurt, believing they can "run out" any problem. Use common sense: if exercise makes your injury hurt more, don't exercise. Never, for example, run on a painful, sprained ankle, hoping to shake the injury. On the other hand, if a small injury, such as a pulled muscle, doesn't hurt during a workout, additional exercise may not cause further problems and might even help. In some cases, a sore spot may not be directly affected by exercise. Running if you have a strained wrist, for example, is usually no trouble.

Generally, you won't go wrong if you listen to your body. It'll let you know if you're pushing too hard.

## Sore Muscles

Everyone, especially people who don't exercise regularly, gets sore muscles occasionally. The day after starting a running regimen, for example, you'll probably discover some aches in your legs. Or, in the case of weightlifting, you may bring a few days of soreness to your pectoral muscles.

Exercise physiologists believe that muscle soreness is mainly caused by hundreds of microscopic tears in muscle tissue, perhaps accompanied by involuntary contractions of some of the muscle fibres. There's also the possibility that some of the lactic acid your muscles produce during exercise remains in the muscles afterwards and causes part of the soreness.

Whatever the reason for sore muscles, you can't completely avoid them, particularly when beginning a fitness course. But if you use care, you can keep these aches and pains to a minimum. For example, always remember to stretch well before you begin a workout. By warming up your muscles beforehand, they'll be better prepared for the more demanding exercises of your workout. Also, go easy at the beginning. If you're running or swimming, keep your distances short. If you're lifting, use light weights at the start of your regimen.

One special type of muscle soreness that people get during the early stages of a running program is called *shin splints*. This is a terrible-sounding name for inflamed muscles and tendons, the tissue that connects muscles to bones. When you have shin splints, you feel tightness and pain along the fronts of your legs and below your knees. Unless the pain is too much to bear, you can continue to run with shin splints. The cause of this ailment is the jolting your legs receive during running, especially when running on hard surfaces and in shoes that lack soft padding. Accordingly, a good pair of running shoes will usually prevent a case of shin splints. Running on soft surfaces, such as the grass in a park, will also help you avoid them.

But when your muscles do get sore, what can you do about it? Unfortunately, not too much. Hot baths soothe sore muscles by keeping them loose and by increasing the blood supply to them. The heat helps repair tissue and to remove lactic acid. Some of the commercial muscle rubs may bring relief also. Unless the soreness is severe (which may indicate a more serious problem, such as a muscle strain), feel free to continue exercising—but with less energy than you might do without soreness. In most cases, it's only a matter of time. After about 3 workout periods, or one week, all soreness will likely be gone.

## Sprains

A sprain is an injury to the muscles and blood vessels surrounding a bone joint or to the tough tissue that binds muscles and bones, the ligaments and tendons. The usual cause is the accidental stretching of a bone joint beyond its normal range of movement.

A good example of a sprain is a twisted ankle, which you may remember as a painful injury. The ankle is the most commonly sprained joint, but the knee, shoulder, elbow, wrist, and even the lower back can all be sprained. Sprains are difficult for your body to repair. They require at least a few days to heal, and sometimes a couple of weeks.

The best treatment for a sprained joint is application of a cold, wet pack to the injured area immediately after the injury has occurred. The cold helps keep the swelling down by restricting the supply of blood to the injured area. A good method for applying the cold pack is to use a plastic bag filled with crushed ice. To protect the skin from the cold ice, cover the ice pack with a thin towel or cloth. These ice treatments should last about a half-hour and be repeated every few hours during the first day after the sprain has occurred. *Do not* use the injured joint for at least a day. After that, limit its use until the pain has greatly decreased and any swelling has gone away. If swelling does not disappear, see your doctor.

## Strains

Any muscle or tendon in your body can be stretched too far and possibly torn. The injury resulting from over-stretching is called a strain. You may know it by the more familiar name of "pulled muscle." Some strains are so severe that they require surgery to repair the damage. Fortunately, most strains are not that serious and heal themselves in due time. A reduced level of exercise on your part is a great aid towards healing.

The best first-aid treatment for a muscle strain is to apply an ice pack to the injured area immediately after the mishap has occurred. Ice treatment can be followed a few hours later by warm soaks and, of course, complete rest for the strained area. As suggested for sprains, you're wise not to use a strained muscle until it is totally healed.

## Cramps

Cramps can occur in almost any muscle, although the legs seem to get them the most. The calf is a common site, as is the hamstring, where cramps are nicknamed "charley horses."

If you experience a cramp, stretch the muscle, using your hands to do the stretching if necessary. Stretching helps because a cramp is an involuntary contraction of a muscle and you must pull it back to its normal condition. Kneading and rubbing the cramped area also helps, and sometimes slapping it will relax the tensed muscle. Above all, *do not* sit down if you get a cramp in your leg. This may make the condition worse.

For a cramp while in the water, remain calm and relaxed and let your buddy or someone else nearby know that you need help. If a leg cramps, try to float on your back and bring the leg up to massage the area. Similarly, for stomach cramps while swimming, lie on your back and massage the area. It may help to bring your knees up to your chest, followed by stretching your legs out.

## Blisters

Blisters are injuries caused by too much rubbing of the skin in one area. Although not a serious medical problem, they can be annoying, painful, and can cost you as many workout days as strains and sprains can.

The best advice for blister care is to prevent them from occurring in the first place. When you run, wear good shoes and soft socks to avoid excessive rubbing of the skin on your feet. When lifting weights, chinning, or climbing ropes, don't work at it so hard that you begin to burn your hands. In time, with regular workouts, you'll develop calluses on your hands that will act as padding and prevent blister development.

If you do get a blister, smear it with a first-aid cream and cover it with adhesive tape and gauze. The skin covering the blister will prevent infection and the annoying blister will probably disappear in a few days. Try to continue your workouts if the blister isn't too painful, and if you can, remove or stop the cause of the blister problem.

On the other hand, if you have a blister that rips open, take care to prevent infection. Wash the area thoroughly, apply antiseptic ointment and tape a gauze pad over the wound. Follow this procedure once a day and carefully watch to see if the injured area is beginning to heal. If it looks like it might be getting infected (swollen, discolored), see your doctor.

Sometimes large blisters are so annoying or painful that they can prevent you from working out. If this happens to you, consider breaking the blister yourself. Wash it well and then drain the blister by puncturing it with a sterile needle. Squeeze out the fluid and treat it as you would a ripped blister: use antiseptic ointment and cover it with gauze.

## Illness

Most of us want to do little more than lie down when sick, particularly when the illness comes equipped with a fever. We certainly don't want to go out and jog or work out with weights. To do so would be both dangerous and uncomfortable, and it wouldn't add to your strength anyway. Your body cannot fight off an illness and build up its muscles at the same time. So if you're sick, *do not work out.*

Once you've recovered from an illness, start your workouts slowly. *Do not* try to do as many reps as you did before you got sick, or try to run or swim as far. Your body requires some time to recuperate from any sickness. It's always a good idea to wait at least 24 hours after a fever has disappeared before resuming even light exercise.

## Questions and Answers

*I twisted my ankle about three months ago and it still hurts every time I run. What can I do to help it heal faster?*

The most important thing you can do is to stop running. You probably didn't give the ankle enough time to heal before you started working out again. Continuously straining your injured ankle can lead to permanent damage, so rest until your ankle is healed completely.

*Do elastic bandages help sprained joints heal?*

Not directly. They help provide extra support to the injured joint, which helps prevent re-injury. It's a good idea to wear one if you insist on working out before all the soreness is gone from the injured area. Always be careful not to wrap an elastic bandage so tightly that it restricts blood circulation.

*Does massage help strained muscles heal faster?*

*Gentle* massage, if administered properly, can help muscles heal faster. If nothing else, it makes the affected area feel better for a while. Massage, however, should be given by someone trained in the technique, such as a physical therapist.

*You claim that no one should work out if he's sick. Does that include mild head colds with no fever?*

It depends on the type of workout and on how you feel. Running outside in cold weather may make your cold worse, but it might make you feel better in warm weather. You have to listen to your body. You can probably lift weights, but *do not* use as heavy a weight as you normally would. You simply don't have your normal strength when you have a cold.

# GLOSSARY

*abdomen*—the general area below your stomach which houses the intestines

*Achilles tendon*—the strong band in back of your ankle which connects the calf muscles to the heel bone

*adipose tissue*—fat which can build up in your body, usually from lack of exercise

*aerobics*—exercises which strengthen your lungs and heart

*agility*—the ability to move quickly and gracefully

*amino acids*—acids containing nitrogen which are the building blocks of proteins

*antibodies*—substances produced by your body to fight disease

*antiseptic*—a substance that kills harmful germs

*attire*—(as used in this book) what you wear during and after exercising

*attitude*—the feelings you have about what you do—a positive attitude is an important part of a good performance

*buddy system*—exercising or playing sports with a friend who knows how to handle emergencies

*calcium & phosphorus*—minerals necessary for strong bones

*carbon monoxide*—a poisonous gas that is produced by incomplete burning of gasoline

*"charley horse"*—a painful cramp in the hamstring muscles

*circulatory system*—the heart, arteries, veins and blood vessels working together to supply your body with blood

*clean*—in weightlifting, this is the upright position in which the barbell is at chest level

*complete proteins*—proteins that contain all eight essential amino acids

*contraction*—a sudden squeezing or tightening feeling in your muscles

*coordination*—the quality of being able to control your muscular action accurately and without awkwardness *deadlift*—lifting the barbell straight up to a standing position with your arms extended down

*digestive system*—the organs and chemicals in your body which convert food into energy the body can use

*environment*—the surroundings and events which affect the kind of life you have

*essential amino acids*—eight amino acids not produced by your body but necessary for proper nutrition

*fatigue*—a state of being tired which lasts longer than usual

*flutter kick*—a kick used in swimming which resembles a short, snappy walking step

*frostbite*—the freezing of part of your body—runners should be careful to avoid frostbite by dressing properly

*hemoglobin*—a substance in the blood which carries oxygen from the lungs to the other parts of your body

*hypertension*—high blood pressure

*hypodermic*—below the outside layer of skin

*isopropyl alcohol*—commonly known as "rubbing alcohol"—soothes tired and sore muscles while sterilizing the skin

*kidney*—an organ located at the base of your backbone which acts to rid the body of waste

*kilocalories*—unit of heat measurement to determine the energy contained in certain foods

*ligaments*—tough tissues which connect one bone to another

*limber*—the flexible, supple feeling that your muscles have when they are completely relaxed

*muscle*—an organ made up of bundles of fibres attached at the end to the bone it controls

*nausea*—a feeling of sickness most often in your stomach—it sometimes causes vomiting

*nutrients*—substances in food that are necessary for life

*obesity*—the condition of being overweight

*optimum*—the best possible conditions

*overtraining*—training without the necessary rest periods—it can actually lead to a *decrease* in strength

*parallel*—lines running in the same direction—for example, train tracks are parallel to each other

*perserverance*—the quality of trying again and again without giving up

*physique*—the outward appearance of your body

*precautions*—any step that you take to avoid harmful situations before they happen

*protein*—the "sovereign nutrient" and the most important in bodybuilding

*psychologist*—a person who studies the human mind and how it affects the way people act

*"pumped up"*—a feeling weightlifters get when their muscles are flooded with blood after a workout

*regimen*—a routine that is part of what you do every day

*respiratory system*—the means by which air is supplied throughout your body by the lungs

*rotations*—turning in a circular motion

*shin splints*—inflammation in muscles and tendons of the legs, usually from overtraining in running

*spotter*—someone who helps the weightlifter, especially in difficult exercises

*stamina*—the ability to keep up an exercise or sport without becoming overtired

*sterile*—free from any bacteria or germs

*tendons*—dense tissue which connects muscles to the bones they control

# INDEX

abdominal muscles, 15, 71-74, 118
Achilles tendon, 38, 39, 40
adipose tissue, 19, 123
aerobics
  benefits of, 35
  bicycling, 52-56
  definition of, 33-35
  general rules, 59-61
  key points, 61
  regimens, 63-64
  rope jumping, 56-59
  running, 35-42, 60
  swimming, 43-52
alcohol, effect of, 8, 20
ankle sprains, 134, 137
arm muscles, 15, 69-71, 107-110
*Australian Weight Lifting Journal,* 87
back muscles, 14, 24, 25, 74-77, 94-97
biceps, 15, 70
bicycling
  equipment, 52-53
  history of, 52
  proper form, 54-55
  regimens, 62
  road hazards, 54
  safety, 53, 54
  speed and distance, 56
*Bike World,* 54
blisters, prevention and treatment, 136-137
calves, 14, 28
*Canadian Cyclist,* 54
carbohydrates, energy from, 123, 129
"charley horses," 135
chest muscles, 15, 24, 25, 69-71, 97-102

cigarette smoking, effect of, 19, 21
circulatory system, 15-16, 35
clean, in weightlifting, 87, 88-90, 96-97
cramps, 135-136
*Cycle Australia,* 54
*Cycling,* 54
deltoids, 15, 70
diet, suggestions for, 127-130
drug addiction, 8
Ender, Kornelia, 43
fats, energy from, 123-124, 129
food supplements, 130
"flyes," 100
gastrocnemius muscles, *see* calves
gluteus maximi, 14
hamstrings, 14, 26-27
heart disease, 8, 19
hypertension, 19
illness, effect on workouts, 137, 138
injuries, 31, 132-133
*International Cycle Sport,* 54
*International Swimmer,* 45
*Iron Man,* 87
Jenner, Bruce, 7
*Jogger's World,* 36
jogging, 20-21, 36
junk foods, 126-127
Kennedy, President John F., 8
kidney disease, 19
lats, 14
leg muscles, 14-15, 27-28, 74-77, 90-93
mental conditioning, 11, 17-18, 20
minerals, benefits of, 125

muscles, 20, 67-69
  abdominal, 15, 71-74, 118
  arms, 15, 69-71, 107-110
  back, 14, 24, 25, 74-77,
    94-97
  chest, 15, 24, 25, 69-71,
    97-102
  composition of, 11-14
  cramps, 135-136
  female development of, 20,
    84-85
  legs, 14-15, 27-28, 74-77,
    90-93
  pulls, 135
  shoulders, 15, 26, 69-71,
    102-106
  soreness, 132-134
  sprains, 134-135
*Muscular Development,* 87
nutrients, definition of,
  122-123
nutrition
  carbohydrates, 123, 129
  fats, 123-124, 129
  fortified and enriched
    foods, 131
  junk food, 126-127
  key points, 127
  minerals, 125
  nutrients, 122-123
  proper diet, 127-130
  protein, 124-125, 130, 131
  vitamins, 125, 130-131
  water, 131
obesity, 8, 19, 123
Olympics, 7, 36,
overeating, effect of, 18-19
pecs, 15, 21, 69
President's Council for
  Physical Fitness, 8
protein, benefits of, 124-125,
  130, 131
"pumping iron," 87
quadriceps, 14-15, 28

*RACE,* 36
reps, 30
respiratory system, 15-16,
  **35**
rope jumping
  advantages of, 56-57
  equipment, 57-58
  proper form, 58
  time devoted to, 58-59
*Runner, The,* 36
*Runner's World,* 36
running
  equipment and clothing,
    36-37
  facilities, 37-38
  history of, 35-36
  injuries, 39
  magazines devoted to, 36
  proper form, 39-40
  regimens, 60
  speed and distance, 40-42
  weather hazards, 38
sets, 30
shoulder muscles, 15, 26,
  69-71, 102-106
sore muscles
  prevention of, 133
  "shin splints," 133-134
  treatment of, 134
Spitz, Mark, 43
sprains
  ankle, 134, 137
  other body parts, 134
  treatment of, 134-135
*Strength and Health,* 87
*Strength Athlete,* 88
strength-building exercises
  advantages of, 67-69
  clothing, 69
  dips, 77-78
  extensions, 74-76
  key points, 78-79
  leg raises, 73-74
  pull-ups, 70-71, 81

push-ups, 69-70
regimens, 79-80, 82-83
rope climb, 78
sit-ups, 71-73
special equipment, 77-78
squats, 76-77
stretching exercises
  benefits of, 23-24
  bridge, 25
  calf stretch, 28
  kick-over, 25
  leg stretches, 27-28
  lunge, 28
  regimens, 30-31
  shoulder rotations, 26
  side bends, 24
  time devoted to, 29-30, 32
  toe touches, 26-27, 31-32
  twisting, 24-25
*Swimmers,* 45
swimming
  breaststroke, 45-46, 50-51
  competitive, 21
  crawl stroke, 45
  equipment and clothing, 44
  freestyle, 50
  history of, 43
  safety, 45
  speed and distance, 51-52
  "swimmer's ear," 44-45
  where to go, 43-44
*Swimming Times,* 45
*Swimming World,* 45
tooth decay, 8
traps, 14
triceps, 15, 69, 109-110
vitamins, benefits of, 125
water, as nutrient, 131

weightlifting
  benefits of, 84-85
  breathing control, 90
  clean, 87, 88-90, 96-97
  clothing, 87
  equipment, 85-87
  key points, 111
  magazines devoted to, 87-88
  "pumping iron," 87
  records, 84
  regimens, 112-119
  safety, 85, 87
  spotters, 87
  time devoted to, 116-117
weightlifting exercises
  bench presses, 97-99
  bent-over lateral raises, 106-107
  bent-over rowing, 94-96
  calf raises, 93
  cleans, 96-97
  curls, 107-109
  deadlifts, 94-95
  front lateral raises, 105-106
  front squats, 91-92
  laterals, 100
  leg extensions, 93
  military presses, 102-104
  narrow-grip bench presses, 109
  pullovers, 100-102
  shoulder shrugs, 96
  side lateral raises, 106
  squats, 90-91
  step-ups, 92-93
  stiff legged deadlifts, 94-95
  triceps extensions, 109-110
  upright rowing, 105